T. Watters

Lao-Tzu

A study in Chinese philosophy

T. Watters

Lao-Tzu
A study in Chinese philosophy

ISBN/EAN: 9783741197888

Manufactured in Europe, USA, Canada, Australia, Japa

Cover: Foto ©Thomas Meinert / pixelio.de

Manufactured and distributed by brebook publishing software
(www.brebook.com)

T. Watters

Lao-Tzu

LAO-TZŬ,

老子

A STUDY

IN CHINESE PHILOSOPHY,

BY

T. WATTERS, M.A.,

Mem. N.C.B. of the Asiatic Society of London, Hon. Mem. Asiatic
Society of Paris, and a Junior Assistant in H.M.'s
Consular Service in China.

————

HONGKONG:
PRINTED AT THE "CHINA MAIL" OFFICE.
1870.

LONDON:
WILLIAMS & NORGATE.

PREFACE.

A CONSIDERABLE portion of the following pages has already appeared in "The Chinese Recorder and Missionary Journal," and its reappearance in its present form requires an apology. The subject of the work is one in which very few take any interest, and the author is very sensible of his numerous imperfections in attempting to deal with matters so difficult and abstruse as are treated of in the Tao-tĕ Ching. Having thus made confession, it only remains for him to thank Mr. Baldwin and his other friends for their kindness in assisting to get the book through the press.

T. W.

FOOCHOW, *October* 19, 1869.

LAO-TZŬ, 老 子

A STUDY IN CHINESE PHILOSOPHY.

CHAPTER I.

INTRODUCTORY.

One of the most remarkable men in the history of China, as also in the history of philosophy, is Lao-tzŭ, the author of the *Tao-té-ching* (道德經). This book deserves, and has obtained with those who know it, a high place among philosophical works, and the posthumous fortunes of its author have very rarely been surpassed. That his own followers—or at least those who professed to be and probably believed that they were his followers—should magnify his name was only what we would have expected. They have raised him from the rank of ordinary mortals, and represented him as an incarnation of deity, showing himself on this earth at sundry times and in various manners. His conception and birth, his personal appearance, and everything about him, have been represented by them as supernatural; and the philosophic little treatise which he composed is regarded as a sacred book. Much of this has arisen from a spirit of rivalry with Buddhism. The Taoists did not wish to be behind the Buddhists in the amount of glory and mystery attaching to the reputed originator of their religion; and they

accordingly tried to make the fortunes of Lao-tzŭ like those
of Shakyamuni, the Buddha of the Present.

Both Confucianists and Buddhists, however, also regard
the *Tao-tĕ-ching* as a book of deep mysteries, and admit the
supernatural, or at least marvellous, character of its author,
though, as will be seen, many censure him for teaching doctrines either in themselves mischievous or leading to evil
results when fully developed. At several periods of Chinese
history Lao-tzŭ has enjoyed the patronage of government,
and almost supplanted Confucius. Indeed, during several'
of the dynasties which reigned within the first few centuries
of our era, there seems to have been a constant struggle
for ascendancy between the followers of these two philosophic chiefs. Emperors have done honour to Lao-tzŭ in his
temple, and the sovereigns of the great Tang dynasty were
proud to deem him their lineal ancestor. One emperor has
even written an excellent commentary on his book; and one
of the best editions of the *Tao-tĕ-ching* as regards textual excellence is that by a Confucian mandarin under the present
dynasty. Buddhist monks also have edited the book with
annotations, and many of them regard it and its author with
a reverence second only to that with which the Taoists regard them.

It is not only, however, his own countrymen who have
given honour to this prophet. By Western writers also
great and mysterious things have been attributed to him.
Some have found in his book an enunciation of the doctrine
of the Trinity. The illustrious Remusat discovered in it
the sacred name Jehovah, and many curious analogies with
the best philosophic writings of ancient times, and more
especially with those of Greece. Pauthier, who has read
and written largely about Lao-tzŭ, finds in his teachings the

triple Brahma of the ancient Hindoos, the Adibuddha of the Northern Buddhists, and an anticipated Christianity. The *Tao* (道) of which Lao-tzŭ speaks so much has been likened to God, to the Logos of Plato and the Neoplatonists, to "the nonentity of some German philosophers," and to many other things. Pauthier says:—"Le dieu invoquè et decrit par *Lao-tseu* est la *Grande Voie* du monde, la *Raison suprême* *universelle* (道) materiellement identique avec le mot qui sert à designer Dieu dans les langues grecque (θεὸς) latine (Deus) et leurs derivées modernes ; mais les attributs qu'il lui donne ne sont point ceux qu'ont donnèes à l'Etre suprême toutes les doctrines spiritualistes de l'Orient, transmises à l'Occident par une voie juive et grecque ; par les therapeutes et les esséniens, dont Jesus, le fils de l'homme, fut le revelateur et le representant à l'etat philosophique."[1] Our missionaries have used this word *Tao* to represent λόγη in their translation of the New Testament, and the first five verses of St. John's Gospel are nearly as much Taoist as Christian in the Chinese text.

Some writers on the other hand, such as Gutzlaff, have represented Lao-tzŭ as writing nonsense, and they seem to insinuate that he did not even know the meaning of what he was writing. Others, as Voltaire, have charged on him all the follies and superstitions practised by the Taoists, and have consequently decried him and his teachings. This is just about as wise and just a proceeding as to reproach the Apostle Paul on account of the sayings and doings of sects like Muckers, and Mormons, and Muggletonians. Many also regard Lao-tzŭ as a mere speculative recluse, shutting himself up from the turmoils and miseries

---

[1] Chine, p. 114.

of social life, and publishing theories in politics and morals
of no practical tendency whatever. In these respects he is
constantly contrasted with Confucius, who is looked upon
as an eminently practical man, teaching to the people only
things which they could easily understand, and ever re-
fusing to wander into the regions of uncertainty and mystery.

There are, so far as I know, very few translations of the
Tao-tĕ-ching in western languages. According to Sir J. F.
Davis, a manuscript copy of a Latin translation is preserved
in the Library of the Royal Society of England. Pauthier
has translated part of the book into French, and has an-
nounced his determination to complete the work. Julien,
however, perhaps the best and soberest of Lao-tzŭ's ex-
pounders, has translated into French the entire book, along
with many Chinese notes and fragments illustrating the
life and teachings of its author. Hegel says there is at
Vienna a translation of the *Tao-tĕ-ching*, or as he calls it
Tao-king, which he himself had seen[2]. He does not, however, mention the name of the translator or the language of
the translation, but I think we are justified in inferring that
it is German. In English we have the recent work of the
Rev. Mr. Chalmers, a missionary and scholar of no ordinary
attainments. He has some excellent remarks in his Introduction, but the translation itself, being almost unaccom-
panied with note or comment, and being apparently made
from a bad text, is rather disappointing. Ritter, Cousin,
Hardwicke, Edkins, and many others have given short
accounts of Taoism; but few of these have clearly separated Lao-tzŭ and his doctrines from the later Taoists and

---

[2] Geschichte der Philosophie, B. 1. p. 142.

their doctrines. The " extravagant vagaries" of the latter
may have arisen often from misinterpreted or misapplied
statements of Lao-tzŭ, but they are not to bo imputed to
him.[3] We must ascribe to Lao-tzŭ only the things which
are his—the merits and defects of his own direct teachings.

[3] Compare Remusat, Mémoire sur la vie et les opinions de Lao-tseu,
&c., p. 20.

CHAPTER II.

THE LIFE OF LAO-TZŬ.

The life of Lao-tzŭ, like the book which he wrote, is enveloped in mystery; and one might almost be excused for doubting whether such a person ever actually existed. One author, indeed, has even gone the length of saying that Lao-tzŭ was made out of space or vacuity (*hung* 洪).[1] The most reliable account of him which has come down to us is that by Szŭ Ma-chien, or Sze-ma-thsien (司馬遷), in the *Shi-chi* (史紀), and this is very brief and unsatisfactory. We have also occasional notices of him in other old books, but the stories told about him in the Records of Spirits and Fairies and works of a like nature are, as Julien observes, only a tissue of falsehoods which all sensible men reject.

Szŭ Ma-chien says[2] Lao tzŭ was a native of the hamlet Ch'u-jen (曲仁) of the parish Lai or Li (厲) in the district K'u (苦), a town of the state Ch'u (楚): his surname was Li (李), his name Erh (耳), his style Po-yang (伯陽) and

---

[1] Tai-p'ing-kwang-chi (太平廣志) ch. 1; and the Shan-hsien-chien, vol. 1.

[2] Shi-chi—老莊申韓列傳三

his posthumous designation Tan (聃).[3] He was in office at the court of Chou (周) as Shou-tsang-shĭ-chĭ-shĭ (守藏室之史), which Julien translates " gardien des archives."

I have been unable to obtain from Chinese sources any reliable statement as to the date of Lao-tzŭ's birth; though Pauthier[4] asserts positively that he was born on the 14th day of the 9th moon, in the year B.C. 604. In this he is followed by Julien, who, however, says candidly—" cette date (the 3rd year of king Ting 定 of the Chou dynasty, corresponding to B.C. 604) que nous insérons ici, est conforme à la tradition historique la mieux établie mais elle ne se trouve point dans la notice du Sze-ma-thsien dont nous donnons la traduction."[5] There is nothing improbable in this date, as we know from other sources that Lao-tzŭ was a contemporary of Confucius, though very much his senior; and as Confucius was born about B.C. 550, Lao-tzŭ must apparently have been born about the beginning of the sixth century B.C. The latter sage indeed, is usually represented as having attained to a very great age, and as having been alive much more than fifty years before the birth of Confucius. Ch'ao, a well known author, quoted by Ma Tuan-lin, says that it was in the forty-second year of the reign of king P'ing (平王) that Lao-tzŭ gave his book to the keeper of the Pass.[6] This would carry him up to the eighth century B.C.,

---

[3] An author named Ch'ên (陳) quoted by Ma Tuan-lin, says that, as Tan means flat-eared, it is not probable that it would be given as a posthumous title. Perhaps it is better to regard it as a name or nickname given to him during life.

[4] Wên-hsien-t'ung-k'ao (文獻通考), Ch. 211.

[5] Chine, p. 111.

[6] Tao-te-king. Introduction, Note 1 on page xia.

king P'ing having commenced to reign about the year B.C.
770. Others [a] mention two teachers of Tao (道) as having
lived during the Chou dynasty, one Lao-tan (老聃) and
another named Lao-lai-tzŭ (老萊子). It is by the name
Lao-tau that Confucius usually refers to Lao-tzŭ, while later
authors often use his surname Li or his name Erh. It must
be remembered also that the Lao-tan mentioned by Confucius is regarded by a few commentators as a different
person from the author of the Tao-té-ching.

Nearly all authorities seem to agree with Szŭ Ma-chien as
to the place of Lao-tzŭ's birth in the feudal dependency
Ch'u (楚).   Under this word Biot has the following remarks
—"Nom d'un ancien royaume de la Chine centrale, à l'epo-
que du Tchun-thsieou. Le centre etait dans l'arrondissement
de Tchi-kiang; la limite nord etoit entre le Kiang et le Hoang-
ho; la limite sud etait au midi du Kiang, mais non bien
determinée." [b]   The district city K'u is also said to have
belonged to the principality of Ch'ên. It stood near the
present Kwei-tê-foo, the most easterly of the cities of Honan;
and the present K'u-yang (苦陽) preserves the house of
Lao-tzŭ and a temple dedicated to his memory.[1] Another
account, however, represents him as having been born in the
district city Po (亳) in the province of Honan.[2] The chief of
Ch'u, like the chiefs of many other states, was at the time of
Lao-tzŭ and Confucius only nominally a feudal dependent of
the king. He was originally a Tzŭ (子) or Viscount, but the
title Wang (王) or king was now usurped in the degenerate

[a] See the 十子全書, the extract from Szŭ Ma-chien.

[b] Dict. Villes et Arrond²., p. 244.

[1] Julien, Tao-te king, Introduction, Note 2 on page xlx.

[2] T'ung-chim-kang-mu, Ch. 41.

days of the Chou rulers who were unable to maintain a strong government.

Of the parents of Lao-tzŭ and of his early years I have not found any record in Chinese books; but Pauthier says that according to historic data his father was a poor peasant who had remained a bachelor up to his seventieth year, when he married a peasant woman of the unromantic age of forty years.[1] Whatever were his circumstances, however, I think we may conclude that Lao-tzŭ was in early life a diligent student of the past history and the institutions of the country, and his obtaining office at the court of Chou was probably a consequence of his learning and abilities.

As to the nature of this office I cannot agree with Pauthier and Julien in calling it that of historiographer, or keeper of the State Archives. The word tsang (藏) means a granary or storehouse, and in a note to a passage in the Li-chi, or Record of Ceremonies, it is explained as the Imperial or National Museum.[2] The Shou-tsang-shi (守藏史) would accordingly be the officer in charge of the Museum, and we must remember that when Confucius went to the Capital of Chou to Lao-tzŭ, he saw in the palace the portraits of the early kings, along with many other relics of antiquity, which possessed him strongly with an idea of the magnificence of the first princes of the dynasty.[3] Dr. Legge also, I find, translates the expression by "Treasury-keeper."[4] The legend in the Records of Spirits and Fairies states that Lao-tzŭ was in the time of king Wĕn a Shou-

1 Chine, p. 112.
2 Li-chi, Ch. 3, Sect. 74, Note.
3 See the Chin-yü (家語), Vol. 1, Ch. 3.
4 Ch. Classics, Vol. 1, Proleg., p. 65.

tsang-shi and under king Wu a *Chu-hsia-shi* (柱下史),[1] this latter term meaning assistant historiographer; and it is not improbable that he may have actually held both these offices in succession under king Ting (定) or king Chien (簡), who reigned in the 6th century B. C.

During the time of Lao-tzŭ's residence at the court of Chou, he was visited by two young gentlemen who had come in a carriage and pair from the distant state of Lu (魯). Their names were Ching-shu (敬叔) and K'ung chiu (孔丘) or Confucius, and they had come to learn from the venerable sage the rites and manners of the olden times. The latter of the two, namely, Confucius, had already been a pupil of Lao-tzŭ, and still remembered his former master with affection and respect. According to Chwang-tzu,[2] however, it was not until he was fifty-one years old that Confucius went to see Lao-tzŭ. He himself when little more than a youth had set out on a converting tour, thinking to induce rulers and people throughout the kingdom to cease from their evil ways and turn to the good old paths of primitive virtue. He did not succeed, however, and he now told his master the sorrowful tale of his disappointment. Lao-tzŭ said to him, "If it be known that he who talks errs by excess in arguing, and that he who hears is confused by too much talk, the way (Tao 道)[3] can never be forgot." According to *Szu Ma-chien*, the Master on another occasion lectured his ambitious disciple as follows: "The men of whom you speak, Sir, have with their bones already all mouldered into dust, and only their sayings abide. More-

1 Kang-hsi's Dictionary. Character *Chu* (柱).
2 See his works, Ch. 5, p. 27, the Tien Yun (天運) Section.
3 Chia Yü, Vol. 1, Ch. 3.

over if the superior man 君子 gets his time, he mounts [his car and takes office] : if he does not get his time, he goes through life like a wisp of straw rolling over sand. I have heard that a good merchant with his treasure house deeply stored seems devoid of resources, and that the superior man of perfect excellence has an outward semblance of stupidity. Do you, Sir, put away your haughty airs and many desires, your flashy manner and extravagant will ; these are all unprofitable to you, Sir ; and this is all I have to say to you."[1] In the *Family Sayings* we read that when Confucius was about to leave *Chou*, Lao-tzŭ gave him as his parting gift a warning against going too far in the public reproval of those who were in authority.[2] From this and the other references made to the intercourse between Confucius and Lao-tzŭ in the Family Sayings and the Record of Rites (禮記), it will be seen that they were on terms of intimate friendship; and though Confucius may have deserved the reproof which, according to *Szu Ma-chien*, Lao-tzŭ administered to him, yet this speech has in it so little of the spirit in which allusion is made to Lao-tzŭ by Confucius or his disciples that I am almost tempted to doubt the story.

I have been unable to find in the Chinese works on this subject a statement of the length of time during which Lao-tzŭ served the king of Chou, of the manner in which he performed his duties, or of the immediate reason of his retirement from office. *Szu Ma-chien* simply says,[3] "He cultivated *Tao* and virtue 修道德, learned to live in

1 Shl chî, Lao-tzu.
2 See Chin Yü, Vol. 1, Ch. 3.
3 Shî chî, 1, c.

seclusion and oblivion as the important thing, resided for a long time in Chou ; when he saw the fortunes of the dynasty going to ruin, he left the country and came to the Pass (關). The keeper of the Pass, by name Yin-hsi (尹 喜), said to him, 'Since you are about to go into seclusion, Sir, you must make me a book.' Hereupon Lao-tzŭ produced his book in two sections containing more than 5,000 characters and declaring the meaning of Tao and Tê (道 德). He then went away, and no one knows his end."

In order to understand the conduct of Lao-tzŭ, in retiring from office in Chou and going into seclusion when he saw its fortunes broken, we must know something of the state of the country at the time. Now the reader of the historical and other works relating to this dynasty will remember what a miserable picture of the kingdom is given in most of them. The hard won territories of king Wu 武 were now subject to his degenerate descendants only in name. The whole country was torn up into petty states, which were always warring with each other. Year by year, army after army, with flaunting banners and gay pennons, passed and repassed through the fields of the people, and left desolation and misery in their track. Fathers and husbands, sons and brothers, were taken away from their homes and their work, and kept in long military service far away from their families. Laxity of morals accompanied this state of civil confusion. Chiefs forgot their allegiance to their princes, and wives their duties to their husbands—usurpers were in the state, and usurpers were in the family. Every little chief was striving with his neighbour for the mastery, and the weak and wicked princes of Chou were unable to overcome them and reduce them to peace and obedience. Men of shining abilities and inordinate ambition rose to power in each state, and, wishing to satisfy their ambition, increased the anarchy of the kingdom. The decree of Heaven was slowly changing, and already, in the time of Lao-tzŭ, "Ichabod" was written up for the princes of Chou. We can now easily see why the philosopher taught that men should not strive, but ever give way; that they should be humble and satisfied with a low condition; that men of virtue and integrity should retire from the dangers and vices of a wicked government; and that no honour should be attached to specious abilities or rare acquisitions. True to his principles, he himself, when the prestige of Chou was lost, and the evil days and evil tongues were becoming more and more evil, withdrew from the court and retired into unenvied obscurity.[1] For this course of action, Confucianists and others have severely censured Lao-tzŭ. We must remember, however, that Confucius himself taught (what he had probably learnt from Lao-tzŭ) that when good principles prevail in a country, the superior man takes office; and that he retires when bad government takes their place. There seem to have been at the time only two courses which an upright and faithful public servant could elect to pursue. He might either take his life in his hands, and try by strong measures to recall his rulers to the path of virtue; or he might establish his own good character, and then withdraw from temptation and corruption. Confucius chose the former course, and ended in disappointment; Lao-tzŭ and many others, as we know from the Lun Yü (論 語), chose the latter course.

1 For the distracted state of China about this period, one may read the Shi Ching, the Tung Chien, Ch'un Ch'iu, the Lun Yü, and other books.

The Pass to which *Sze Ma-chien* represents Lao-tzŭ as
going, and where he met with *Yin-hsi* 尹喜, is said in a
note to this passage to be probably *Han-ku-kwan* 函谷關,
the present Ling-pao 靈寶, in the extreme west of Honan,
and on the south bank of the Yellow River. The Pass and
its keeper have since become famous in the legendary and
poetic literature of China. This is the last historical notice
that we have of Lao-tzŭ. He left the Pass, having enriched
the keeper with the 81 chapters he had composed on *Tao*
and Virtue, and went away. "No one knows his end."
We may hope, however, that he died a peaceful, happy
death, in a good old age, having attained a clear insight into
the nature of *Tao* 道 and *Tĕ* 德.

According to the Lao-tzŭ Lie Chuan 老子列傳 of
Sze Ma-chien,[1] Lao-tzŭ left a son named Tsʻung 宗, who
became a high military officer under the chief of Wei 衛,
and was appointed to the feudal dependency Tuan-kan 段
干. His descendants were living in the time of the Han
漢 dynasty in the 2d century B. C.

Such is the sum of the probably true information which
I have succeeded in obtaining about this remarkable man.
Many things that we would have liked to know about him
are wanting, and part of what we have seems uncertain. In
his birth and in his death he was mysterious, and through
all his life he seems to have courted obscurity. He tells us
himself that he appeared to mankind stupid and helpless,
but that he had within himself precious treasures of which
the world did not know.[2] To me he seems to have been a
kind and gentle old philosopher, who thought more of what

1 See 十子全書, Introduction.
2 Tao-tĕ-ching, Chs. 20 and 67.

was beyond this world than about what was in it. I cannot find in him those traits of moroseness and cynicism which others have found, nor any trace of the jealousy and spite with which he is said to have regarded Confucius.[1] Chu-hsi (朱熹) or Chu fu tzŭ, represents him as a man stand-ing aloof from the ordinary ways of men, loving neither their sounds nor their sights, and not living an official life.[2] Confucius himself refers to Lao-tzŭ with affectionate respect, and quotes his opinions as sufficient answers to the questions of his own disciples. He speaks of him as extensively read in antiquity and acquainted with the present, as having penetrated to the sources of Rites and Music, and as under-standing what belonged to Tao and Tĕ (道德之歸).[3] The old man who thought that in troubled times, like those in which they were living, men of wisdom and virtue ought not to make a display of those qualities, but rather to appear to the world destitute of them, when he found his former pupil parading the kingdom with a crowd of disciples (one of whom acted as his car driver), going from court to court admonishing and scolding the chiefs, thought it his duty to give the youthful reformer a sharp reproof and an earnest warning. His advice was excellent, and Confucius found out at last that the restoration of peace and good government to a country was not to be effected so easily as he had thought, even though the preacher of reform dressed unimpeachably, ate and drank only the best he could get, had an excellent ear for music, and knew the decrees of Heaven.

1 See, for instance, a very unfair article on Confucius in the *Fortnightly Review* for May, 1868, by Sir J. Bowring.

2 朱子全書, Ch. 59.

3 Chia Yü (家語), Ch. 3.

I shall now proceed to give a short sketch of the legendary account of Lao-tzŭ, as related in the Records of Spirits
and Fairies and other books.

According to some writers Lao-tzŭ was a spiritual being,
eternal and self-existing, manifesting himself as a human
being on the earth at various times and under various
names. One author, indeed, puts words like these into the
mouth of the sage himself.[1] The most celebrated of his in-
carnations was that which occurred during the early part of
the Chou dynasty. On this memorable occasion his mother,
who had conceived by the influence of a shooting star,
brought him forth under a Li (李) or plum tree, a circumstance from which he derived his surname. For seventy-
two long years (or, according to a more cruel author, for
eighty-one years) had he remained in the wretched woman's
womb, and at last he delivered himself by bursting a passage under his mother's left arm. From his having at his
birth gray hairs and the general appearance of an old man,
he was called the *Old Boy* (Lao-tzŭ 老子)[2]; though some
have conjectured that this was the name of his mother's
family, which was given to the child because his mother
obtained him in an improper manner. One writer says that
Lao-tzŭ could speak immediately on being born, and that
he himself intimated at the time that the plum tree under
which he emerged into the world would furnish his name.
Another says that so soon as he was born he mounted nine
paces in the air—his step producing a lotus flower—and
while poised there, he pointed with his left hand to heaven
and with his right hand to earth, saying: " In Heaven above

---

1 See the Yuan-chien-lei-han (淵鑑類函), Ch. 318.
2 Chalmers translates this " old philosopher."

and on earth beneath it is only Tao which is worthy of
honour. The same author remarks that Shâkyamuni on his
birth rose seven paces in the air, and pointing in a similar
manner to heaven and earth pronounced himself alone
worthy of honour. He observes very properly that there
ought not to be such a coincidence.

When his mother got an opportunity of examining her
wonderful child, she found him a veritable prodigy. Not
only had he gray hairs, but he had also very large ears.
Hence came his name Ěrh (耳), that is, Ears, or as others
give it Chung-ěrh (重耳), Heavy ears. [3] Each ear termi-
nated in a point and had three passages. Besides these
peculiarities the infant had handsome eyebrows—large eyes
—a double-ridged nose—square mouth with thick lips.
His hands had ornamental inscriptions on them, and the
soles of his feet presented the mysterious numbers, two and
five, of which the former represents heaven and the latter
earth. He had also many other larger and smaller bodily
virtues and beauties. [4]

Lao-tzŭ left heavenly purity and honour for earthly pol-
lution and office. It was under the Heaven-blessed kings
Wên (文王) and Wu (武王) that he first took service
in the state as Treasury keeper and then as Assistant historiographer. This account, however, would make him
survive for the more than patriarchal period of five hundred
years. He is represented as having several interviews with

3 See the Records of Spirits and Fairies. Art. 老子. Julien
has translated this Chapter in the Introduction to his Tao-tě Ching.

4 See 老子志略 in the 十子全書. Also compare
the similar legends about the Buddha in Hardy's Manual of Buddhism,
pages 367-8-9.

Confucius who, as Szŭ Ma-chien also relates, compared him to a dragon which in a mysterious and inexplicable manner mounts a cloud and soars into heaven. This, as Rémusat has observed, was intended as a compliment, the dragon being with the Chinese a symbol of what is exalted and not unattended by a mysterious power.[4]

On retiring from office Lao-tzŭ proceeded westward intending to pass through the Han-ku-kwan (函谷關) to the Kunlun mountains and other distant places. Yin-hsi (尹喜), however, the keeper of the pass, who had known from the state of the weather that a sage was to come his way, recognised Lao-tzŭ for such and detained him until he had himself learned Tao. The time came, however, when the two worthies had to part. Lao-tzŭ informed Yin-hsi that he would have to leave him and go away on a long wandering through the boundless realms of space. Yin-hsi begged earnestly that he might be allowed to go with him— saying that he was prepared to follow the Great Genius through fire and water above the heavens and beneath the earth. Lao-tzŭ declined the offer, but presented his old friend with five thousand words on Tao and Tê.

The pathetic state of affairs was now rudely interrupted. Just as Lao-tzŭ was about to take his departure it was found that his old servant Hsü-chia (徐甲), who had attended him for more than two hundred years without pay, seeing Lao-tzŭ about to set out on an apparently unlimited pilgrimage, demanded payment. The arrears of wages due to him amounted to 7,200,000 cash, and he applied to a friend who got Yin-hsi to speak to the sage. This friend gave his handsome daughter in marriage to Hsü-chia, who was quite

4 See his Mémoire sur la vie &c, de Lao-tseu, ps. 5 & 6.

delighted with the arrangement. Just at this time, however, the master appeared and told Chia that he ought to remember from what a poor condition he had been raised, and that he would have been dead long ago had it not been for the charm of long life which had been given to him. He also informed Chia that, as he had previously promised, he had intended to pay the debt in gold on reaching An-hsi (安息), a country which Biot identifies with that of the Parthians. Yielding to the last vestige of earthly infirmity Lao-tzŭ became angry and ordered Chia to fall on his face to the ground and open his mouth. The latter could not but obey, he fell to the ground, the charm came forth fresh as when it was swallowed, and Chia lay like a shrivelled mummy. Through the kindness of Yin-hsi, who recognised the miraculous power of Lao-tzŭ, and knocked his head on the ground to him, the ungrateful creditor was restored to life by the same wondrous charm. Yin-hsi also paid him on behalf of Lao-tzŭ the generous sum of 2,000,000 cash, and sent him away.

Lao-tzŭ having now settled all his mundane affairs, bade farewell to the keeper of the Pass, telling him that he would return to earth after the lapse of a thousand days and that he would be recognised by the sign of a Ching Yang (青羊), literally, an azure sheep. He then mounted a cloud and soared out of sight of the weeping Yin-hsi in a dazzling glare of light away into the etherial regions, to his home in the heavens. [6]

6 One author, however, represents him as travelling far away to the West and becoming again incarnate as Gotama Buddha—see Yuan-chien &c., ch. 317.

CHAPTER III.

THE TAO-TÊ CHING 道 德 經.

Lao-tzŭ is said to have died at the age of eighty-one years
in B.C. 523,[1] though, as has been seen, nothing is known
positively about the time or manner of his decease. He had,
according to historical tradition, on leaving the Hanku Pass,
consigned his writings on Tao and Tê to Yin-hsi, the guar-
dian of the Pass. This latter seems to have transmitted his
doctrines to others, more especially to Wên-tzŭ (文 子),
who probably published the first edition of this work known
to the public. Some indeed suppose that Lao-tzŭ did not
himself commit anything to writing, and that Yin-hsi merely
related orally to Wên-tzŭ and others what he had been
taught orally by the sage. This opinion will not seem un-
likely, if we consider that the use of paper was at this time
unknown and that there were very few facilities of any kind
for publishing a book. Others suppose that Wen-tzŭ was
an immediate disciple of Lao-tzŭ and that he published an account of his master's doctrines after the decease of the latter.[2]

1 Le Livre des Récompenses et des Peines &c., par S. Julien Avertis-
sement, p. 6.

2 Wân-hsien &c, ch., 211.

In any case, however, it appears certain that for a considerable time after the death of its author the work which is now known as the Tao-tê ching remained in at least partial obscurity. Mencius does not allude by name to Lao-tzŭ or his teachings, though he refers on several occasions, and rather unfavorably, to Yang-chu (陽朱), who is supposed to have been a disciple of the sage. The philosophers Chwang (莊) and Lie (列), however, contemporaries of Mencius, seem to have been aware of the existence and contents of the Tao-tê ching. The latter expressly quotes its words, and both make mention of Lao-tan.

It has not been ascertained when or by whom its present title was imposed on this book. We find early writers quoting its teachings as those of Hwang-Lao (黃老), that is, of the Emperor Hwang and Lao-tzŭ. The former lived, or is supposed to have lived, about B.C. 2600, and some parts of the Tao-tê ching are expressly ascribed to him, for example, Chapter VI. is quoted as his.[3] Another title under which this book is referred to by old authors is Lao-tzŭ-shu (老子書), that is, the writings of Lao-tzŭ,[4] and it is not until the time of Emperor Wên (文帝) of the Han dynasty, or about B. C. 160, that we find the term Tao-tê used. We must remember also that the use of these two words does not indicate that the book treats only of what is meant by them,[5] nor are we to imagine that the former part of the work refers exclusively to Tê. The first word of

8 See Lie-tzŭ's Chung-hsü-chên-ching (沖虛真經) Tien-sui (天瑞) ch. where it forms part of a quotation from Hwang Ti's writings.

4 See Julien's Tao-tê-king, p. xxxiii.

5 Hsü Ta-ch'ên's Preface to his edition of the Tao-tê ching.

the former part of the book is Tao, and the first important
word of the latter portion is Tê, and these two were simply
combined in order to form a designation for the whole, according to the usual Chinese custom.[6] Hüan-tsung (玄
宗), an Emperor of the T'ang dynasty, who reigned in the
early part of the 8th century of our era, besides several
other innovations, gave a separate name to each part of this
book, calling the former part the Tao-ching and the latter
the Tê-ching.[7] These appellations, however, are seldom, if
ever, used, and the work is now universally known as the
Tao-tê ching. From the words of Confucius it might even
with some degree of probability be inferred that already in
his time the name Tao-tê was used, the term Ching or
classic, being, of course, a much later addition and given by
way of respect.

From the naming of the book I now proceed to the con-
siderations of the way in which it has been divided. Szŭ
Ma-chien simply says that Lao-tzŭ made a book in two parts,
containing more than five thousand characters, and setting
forth the signification of Tao and Tê. Ch'ao, however, says
that the work contained 5,748 words in eighty-one chapters.
The original division was probably only one into two parts;
afterwards, however, these were subdivided into chapters.
The number of these latter composing the entire book varies
considerably.[8] Some editors make fifty-five chapters; some
make sixty-four; some, and notably Wu-ch'êng, make sixty-
eight; and some seventy-two. The most usual number,

6 See Wu-Ch'ăng's (吳澄) Tao-tê ching, ch. 1.

7 Hsü Ta-chün's edition, Prolegomena 2. This statement, however,
cannot be verified.

8 See Hsü Ta-ch'ün as above.

however, is eighty-one, and this is said to be sanctioned by
the old and venerable authority of Ho-shang-kung(河上公)
of the Han dynasty. The Taoists are very fond of the number three and its multiples, and this particular multiple,
eighty-one, is associated in tradition with Lao-tzŭ's birth
and the years of his life, and there is perhaps no greater
reason for preferring this to any other division.

To Ho-shang-kung is ascribed also the addition of a title
to each of the eighty-one chapters. These titles consist of
two characters each, giving an epitome of the contents of
the chapter, and they resemble the headings of chapters and
sections in our own books. Many editors, however, reject
these inventions of Ho-shang-kung, and use the ordinary
Chinese method of distinguishing each chapter by its first
two characters. This is considered the more decorous method, as the other seems to be supplementing the author.

I come now to the text of the Tao-tĕ ching, and here the
most bewildering uncertainty and confusion are found. Some
editors, wishing to have the number of characters as little as
possible beyond five thousand, have cut them off apparently
at pleasure, and without much regard for the sense of the
author. Others have pursued a contrary course, and re-
tained or added characters in order apparently to make out
what they deemed to be the true meaning of any particular
passage. This conduct has occasioned great variations in
the text, and consequently great uncertainty as to what
Lao-tzŭ actually wrote or taught. Sometimes one editor,
by the suppression of a negative particle or a word of inter-
rogation, gives to a passage a meaning unlike or even opposed
to that which another editor by the insertion of this character gives to the same passage. But not only do different
editions of this book vary as to insertion and rejection of

words: they also differ as to the mode of writing many of
those actually employed. Words written in similar manners,
or of similar sound, but with widely different significations,
frequently replace one another; and not unfrequently characters totally different in sound, appearance, and meaning
are found substituted one for another in the same passage.
Hence the number of various readings is exceedingly great,
and the meaning of many passages at least very doubtful.
One edition gives in the introduction an account of some of
the variations in the text, which occupies a considerable
number of pages; while another edition gives only a text
accompanied by various readings.

The next point to be considered is the style of our author.
This is perhaps the most terse and concise ever employed.
There is little, if any, grace or elegance about it: and most
of the chapters seem to be merely notes or texts for philosophical discourses. They are composed of short and often
enigmatical or paradoxical sentences—not in verse, as has been
asserted[9]—and with a connexion either very slight or not at
all perceptible. Much of the present obscurity may be due
to the antiquity of the language and the uncertainty about
the proper reading; but much is also due to the brief enigmatical manner in which the author has expressed himself.
Many Chinese regard the style as profound and suggestive,
and so, no doubt, it is; but we can never get at the bottom
of the meaning, nor imagine all that is suggested.

Connected with the obscurity of the style, and indeed
contributing largely towards it, is the nature of the topics
discussed. The origin of the universe, and man's place and
destiny in it as an individual, a member of society, and a

9 Panthier, Chine, p. iii.

conscious part of nature, are subjects which in all ages and in all countries have puzzled the minds of thoughtful men, and it is of these and similar matters that Lao-tzŭ principally treats. Such subjects, even when discussed in a clear and plain style and with a rich language, are found to be difficult of elucidation; and how much more so must they be when discussed in short enigmatical sentences? Lao-tzŭ, like all other philosophers who live and write in the infancy of a literary language, had only a very imperfect medium through which to communicate his doctrines. The language of his time was rude and imperfect, utterly unfit to express the deep thoughts of a meditative mind, and hence it could at best but "half reveal and half conceal the soul within."

The genuineness and sources of this book are also difficult of investigation, and it is perhaps impossible to ascertain the truth about them with any accuracy. As has been seen, a portion is ascribed to the semi-fabulous Emperor Hwang, and Lao-tzŭ is sometimes represented as merely transmitting this emperor's doctrines. Chapter XXXI. has been declared spurious, and a portion of Chapter XXVII. is found first in Ho-shang-kung's edition.[1] The beginning of the now famous Chapter XIV. is very similar to the words ascribed to the predecessor of the Emperor Hwang, namely the Emperor Yen (炎), by the philosopher Chwang. Rémusat and Pauthier consider the main doctrines of the Tao-tê ching to be derived from Western sources. The former asks—Did Lao-tzŭ learn them from the Jews or from some oriental sect unknown to us?[2] but the illustrious savant was unable to give a satisfactory answer. The learned Pauthier thinks that Lao-

1 Wĕn-hsien &c., ch. 211.
2 Mémoire &c., p. 49.

tzŭ borrowed his doctrines either from the writings of some
of the ancient Chinese sages or from some Indian philosophers.[3] In Ma-tuan-lin's great work a short account is
given of an ancient worthy named Yŭ-hsuing (鬻熊), who
served the celebrated Wên-wang, and who must accordingly
have flourished about B.C. 1150.[4] This man seems to have
anticipated Lao-tzŭ in certain doctrines, but we have very
little information about him, and what we have can scarcely
be called reliable. Lao-tzŭ never alludes to a previous author; but there cannot be much doubt, I think, that he was
well acquainted with the history and traditions of his country.

We may probably now understand the nature of the
difficulties attending the reading and interpreting of the
Tao-tě Ching, of which western writers have complained.
Julien speaks of it as "cet ouvrage mémorable qu'on regarde
avec raison comme le plus profond, le plus abstrait et le plus
difficile de toute la littérature Chinoise."[5] Rémusat and
Pauthier have written in a similar manner, and the study
of a few pages of the work will show how real are the
difficulties of which they complain. But it is not to foreign
students alone that these difficulties are perplexing; they
are so to the native student also. Some of its editors are
accused not only of not appreciating its spirit, but even of
not understanding its language.

The number of those who have edited and commented on
this work is very great, embracing Buddhists, Taoists, and
Confucianists. The curious reader will find a list of many
of these in the Observations Détachées prefixed to Julien's

3 China Moderne, p.f 350, and Chine, p. 95 &c.
4 Ch., 211.
5 Tao-tě ching, p. ii.

translation. To this list many more names might be added,
but it includes nearly all the useful and well known editions. It is only necessary here to enumerate a few of the
more important and celebrated editions, and those which are
apparently not mentioned by Julien and which have come
under my notice.

1. The Tao-tĕ-ching-chu (道德經註) by Ho-shang-
kung, or as Ma-tuan-lin names the book, Ho-Shang-Kung-
Chu-Lao-tzŭ, may be regarded as the earliest edition of
which we have now any exact information. This Ho-shang-
kung lived in the second century B. C., during the reign of
King Wên (文帝) of the Han dynasty. He derived his
name from his living as a studious hermit on the bank of a
river in a grass-made hut, and neither his original name nor
anything else scarcely is known of him, though Julien calls
him "Lo-chin-kong." To him, as has been seen, is ascribed
the division of Lao-tzŭ's book into eighty-one chapters, as
also the addition of the two-word heading of each chapter.
The original work is said to have been long since lost, and
the professed reprints are now generally regarded as spurious. Many modern editions, however, present what they
designate Ho-shang-kung's text, and Julien seems to regard
himself as possessing the genuine commentary. The edition
of the Tao-tĕ Ching, which forms the first volume in the
Shĕ-tzŭ-ch'uan-shu (十子全書) published during the
reign of Chia-Ch'ing of the present dynasty, professes to give
Ho-shang-kung's text, revised by two scholars of the Ming
dynasty. Later editors are divided in their opinions of the
merits of the recluse's commentary and arrangement of the
text. Some regard the commentary as a fair exponent of
Lao-tzŭ's teachings, while others—and these I think the
majority—regard it as very bad and evincing an ignorance

of the author's meaning. The text which is ascribed to him seems to be freer from obscurities than that of some later editions, but he is accused of having taken great liberties with the words of the original.

2. The edition of Wang-Pi (王弼). This man was the author of the Lao-tzŭ-liao-lun (老子略論), according to Ch'ao. He was a native of Shan-yang (山陽) in the time of the Chin dynasty, which reigned over China in the third and fourth centuries of our era.[6] His style was Szŭ-fu (嗣輔), and he was an early and devoted student of Lao-tzŭ. Besides this, and that he wrote a commentary on the Tao-té chin, and one on the Yi-ching, and died at the early age of twenty-four, much regretted by his sovereign, we know little about Wang-Pi. The text which he gives in his edition is very good, and his notes are very brief. They are, however, in some cases almost as difficult to comprehend as the passages they are intended to explain; though their author is regarded by many as a better student of Lao-tzŭ than Ho-shang-kung, and Mr Wylie says that his commentary is "generally esteemed for its depth of thought and chasteness of diction."[7] He also divided the work into eighty-one chapters. In the 40th year of Chièn-lung, or in 1775, a revised edition of this work was printed in the palace, under the care of three mandarins, who have written a neat little preface to the book. This edition is valuable as giving the variations of Wang-Pi's notes which appeared in the great Encyclopedia known as Yung-lo-ta-tien (永樂大典).

3. The Tao-téching-shi-yi (道德經釋義). This

6 See the Shang-yu-lu (尚友錄), Ch. 9, art. 王.

7 Notes on Chinese Literature, p. 179.

was the work of Lü-yen (呂 嵒), better known as Lü-T'ung-
p'in or Lü-tsu, a famous Taoist of the Tang dynasty. His
commentary is very diffuse, and does not tend very much to
give a clear conception of Lao-tzŭ's views. Many Chinese
scholars, however, believe that the genuine work is not
extant, and that all the editions purporting to be from his
pen are spurious. Lü-yen was also the editor of a Taoist
book written by a celebrated individual of the Han dynasty,
and he was the author of a number of original pieces. He
was promoted to the rank of a Genius, and he is enrolled
as one of the Pa-hsien (八仙) or Eight Genii, under the
style Shun-yang-chên-jen (純楊眞人) ; and in the 29th
year of Kang-hai, Mou-Mu-yuen (牟目源) published an
edition of the Tao-tĉ Ching purporting to be a revised edition
of this man's work. It is a very useful book, giving in addition to the commentary a list of various readings, the sounds
of the rare or doubtful characters, and other valuable information. This is the edition, apparently, to which Julien
refers as a work "publiée en 1690 par Chun-yang-tchin-jin
qui renferme toutes les rêveries des Tao-sse modernes."[8] I
cannot understand, however, how a sinologue of M. Julien's
erudition could mistake the date of the famous Lü-T'ung-pin
or forget that he was identical with Shun-yang-chên-jen.
A new edition of Mou-Mu-yuen's book was published
in the 14th year of Chia-ch'ing (1809) by Tsou-Hsü-k'un
(鄒學組).

4. The edition with notes by Su-Che (蘇轍), a relation of the famous poet and author of the Sung dynasty,
named Su also. Che, or as he is also called Tsŭ-yu, seems
to have been an eclectic philosopher, and he has incurred

8 Tao te, &c. Observations Détachées, p. xxxix.

severe censure from rigid Confucianists for daring to pre-
sume that the doctrines of Shâkyamuni and Lao-tzŭ could
resemble those of their Master. His commentary is written
in a liberal and generous spirit, and shews, besides, a considerable amount of reading, much in advance of ordinary
Chinese authors.

5. Another edition of the Tao-tê Ching, published during
the Sung dynasty, was that of Lü-Tung-lai (呂東萊) or
Tsu-ch'ien (祖謙), also known as Pei-kung (伯恭). He
was a very learned Confucianist, and wrote, along with other
works, an excellent commentary on the Ch'un-ch'iu (春秋)
of Confucius.

6. The Tao-tê-chên-ching-chu (道德眞解註) by
Wu-Ch'êng (吳澄). This man was a native of Lin-chieaa-
hsien (臨川縣) in Kiangsi, and lived under the Yuan or
Mongol dynasty. He divided the Tao-tê Ching into sixty-
eight chapters by putting, in several instances, two or more
of the ordinary chapters into one. His commentary is one
of the best and of the most popular among the Chinese
literati. This is partly owing to the fact that Wu-Chêng
was also a well-known Confucianist and a commentator on
the classics. His style was Yu-ch'ing (幼淸), and it is
under the name Oi-yeou-thsing that Julien makes mention
of him. In Chinese books he is also frequently quoted as
Ts'ao-lu (草廬). A new edition of Wu-Ch'êng's excellent
work appeared in the eighth year of Chia-ch'ing (1803)
with a preface by Chang-Wên-ping, and another edition with
a short supplement appeared in the reign of the late emperor.

7. Under the Ming dynasty there were several good
editions of this work published, but I have been able to
obtain only two of them. The Tao-tê-hsing-ming-ch'ien-chi
(道德性命前集) was published during the reign of

Yung-lo in the first quarter of the 15th century. The editor does not reveal his name but uses a *nom de guerre*, and I have not succeeded in ascertaining anything about his history. The commentary which he has written is very useful, and evinces a careful study of his author and a familiar acquaintance with Chinese literature. The text and the headings of the Chapters are said to be after Ho-shang-kung, and the number of the chapters is eighty-one.

8. The Tao-tê-hsing-ming-hou-chi (道德性命後集) appeared in the reign of Chia-ching (嘉靖) of the same dynasty, and nearly a century after the above edition. The author of this commentary was Chu-Ch'ên-hung (朱宸洪), a relative of the royal family, and a military viceroy with full powers for some time. His notes are short and not of great utility, but he occasionally introduces quotations from early writers illustrative of passages in Lao-tzŭ's teachings, and he seems to have been a man of no mean literary attainments.

9. The Tao-tê Ching, with Prolegomena and Commentary by Hsü-Ta-ch'un (徐大椿), was published in 1760. Ta-ch'un's style was Ling-t'ai (靈胎), and he was born in Wu-chiang-hsien (吳江縣) in the department of Soochow, in the reign of Yung chêng. He was well-known during his life as an accomplished scholar, and a writer on medicine and other subjects. His commentary on the Tao-tê Ching is to be reckoned among the most useful of all the commentaries that have hitherto appeared. He speaks very slightingly of previous editors, more especially of Ho-shang-kung, and he advertises his readers that he has not stolen anything from his predecessors, but has studied his author. Mr. Wylie says that Ta-ch'un in this commentary, "in a concise and lucid style, developes his ideas on the

work of Lahu-tze, extolling it above the Confucian Classics."⁹

10. The Tao-tê-ching-k'ao-yi (道德經攷異) by Pi-Yuan (畢沅), a high officer under Chien-lung. He published this work in the forty-sixth year of this reign (1781) in two volumes, and with the chapters divided in the usual manner. The text which he gives is that settled by Fu-yi (傅奕), an imperial annalist during the T'ang dynasty, and his notes consist almost exclusively of an enumeration of the variations presented by previous editions. Mr Wylie speaks of it as "a very excellent examination of the purity of the text,"¹ but it is scarcely so much as a statement of the various readings, with an occasional attempt at explanation or reconciliation.

11. The Lao-tzŭ-ts'an-chu (老子參註). Of this Mr. Wylie writes:—"A critical exposition of the work (that is, of the Tao-tê Ching) was written by 倪元垣 E Yuên-t'ăn in 1816, entitled the 老子參註 Laou-tszè-ts'an-choó."²

Appended to several editions of the Tao-tê Ching is a small tract bearing the name Yin-fu Ching (陰符經), that is, as explained by one author, the Classic of the Secret Tally. It contains only a few sentences, generally obscure and enigmatical, bearing on subjects similar to those treated of by Lao-tzŭ. The author of the work is unknown, and some refer it to the ancient Hwang-Ti (about B. C. 2630), while others bring it down so late as Li-Ch'uan (李筌) of the

⁹ Notes on Chinese Literature, p. 173. I have failed, however, to verify the concluding part of the sentence.

1 Notes, &c , p. 173.

2 Notes, &c., p. 174.

Tang dynasty.[3] It seems more probable, however, that it was written by Tai-kung (太公), who is also known as as Lü-wang (呂望) and Chiang-shang (姜尚). He was feudal chief of the principality of Ch'i (齊), and lived under kings Wên and Wu of the Chou dynasty (about B. C. 1150 to 1120). Szŭ-ma-ch'ien[4] mentions the book under the title Chou-shu-yin-fu (周書陰符), as having been studied by Su-Ch'in (蘇秦), a famous general about the time of Mencius, who attained to the high position of chief minister for six of the seven states then contending; hence he is frequently spoken of as Liu-kuo-hsiang (六國相). The Yin-fu-Ching forms part of the curious book called the Magnetic Needle (指南針), where the text is accompanied with very interesting notes.

3 Notes, &c., p. 173.
4 Shi-chi, Ch. 8.

CHAPTER IV.

GENERAL VIEW OF LAO-TZŬ'S TEACHINGS.

Before proceeding to examine in detail the doctrines of the *Tao-tĕ Ching*, I shall briefly indicate their general nature; and by way of preface to my own remarks, I now present to the reader the statements of two critics of different countries, and of rather widely separated dates. One of these, *Chu-hsi* 朱熹, a Chinese philosopher who lived in the 12th century, says:—"Lao-tzŭ's scheme of philosophy consists in modesty, self-emptiness, the saving of one's powers, and the refusal in all circumstances to agitate the bodily humours and spirits. Lao-tzŭ's learning consists, generally speaking, in being void of desires, quiet, and free from exertion—in being self-empty, retiring, and self-controlling (lit., self-keeping) in actual life. Accordingly, what his words are ever inculcating is to have in outward deportment a gentle tenderness and modesty, and to be at the core void of all selfishness, and unhurtful to all things in the world."[1] The other critic, a French philosopher still living, says:—"La conception de *Lao-tseu* est un Rationalisme panthéistique absolu dans lequel le monde sensible est considéré comme la cause

1 Collected Writings, ch. 58.

de toutes les imperfections et de toutes les misères, et la
personalité humaine comme un mode inférieur et passager
du grand Être, de la grande *Unité*, qui est l'origine et la fin
de tous les Êtres. Elle a, comme nous l'avons déjà dit ailleurs
une grande analogie avec le système de l'*Identité absolue* de
Schelling. Il y a cette différence, cependant, que la conception du premier n'est en quelque sorte qu'à l'état rudimentaire,
comme la civilization de son époque, tandis que le système du
dernier embrasse tous les progrès que la pensée philosophique a fait pendant plus de deux mille ans d'incessants et
souvent d'infructueus labeurs."[2] I am unable to coincide
perfectly with the opinions of the above critics, especially
with those of the latter; and I shall probably refer to them
again. There is at least one respect in which the writings
of Lao-tzŭ resemble those of Schelling—that is, in being
frequently quite unintelligible to all ordinary mortals.

Pauthier, however, seems to have observed what the Chinese critic apparently failed to notice—namely, that all Lao-
tzŭ's teachings are the elucidation and development of his
idea of the relations between something which he names *Tao*
and the Universe. In taking a general view of Lao-tzŭ's
philosophy, this is the first observation I have to make:—It
is a system which refers all things to *Tao*, as the ultimate
ideal unity of the universe. The sum of the *Tao-té Ching* may
be said to be that *Tao* originated all things, is the everlasting
model of rule for all things, and that into it all things are
finally absorbed. It behoves us then, at the outset, to endeavour to ascertain what that is which Lao-tzŭ designates
by this name, and to find some sort of an equivalent for it
in our own language, if possible.

2 Chine Moderne, p. 351.

Now the character *Tao* 道 is used in several very different
senses in the *Tao-tĕ Ching*. (1) It is used in the sense of the
way or means of doing a thing.[3] (2) In some passages it
means to speak of or describe.[4] (3) It is used in the sense
of the course—literal and metaphorical—characteristic of
and pursued by Heaven, Earth, the perfect man, &c.[5] This
usage of the word is common to Lao-tzŭ with the Confucianists
and all other Chinese writers. In some places also it seems
to be used in the sense of good principles—truth—as in Confucianist writings. (*See Ch.* 46.). (4) There is the transcendental use of the word, perhaps originated by Lao-tzŭ,[6]
but at least chiefly transmitted through him. It is with *Tao*
used in this last sense alone that we have to deal at present,
and I shall accordingly now give a sketch of Lao-tzŭ's own
account of the *Tao* which has given a name to his philosophy.

Tao, then, is something which existed before heaven and
earth were, before Deity was, and which is, indeed, eternal.[7]
It has not any name really,[8] and it never had a name; but
Lao-tzŭ feels himself obliged to devise an epithet for it,
and he adopts the word *Tao*. This word, however, is not to
be taken in any of its ordinary significations,[9] but is used
in a peculiar sense, to denote that which would otherwise be
nameless. This *Tao* cannot be apprehended by any of the

3 Ch. 59.

4 Ch. 1. This passage is, however, also rendered according to the
metaphor of a road. See Wu-ch'ĕng's note.

5 Chs. 47, 49, 73, 77.

6 See Ch. 25.

7 Chs. 25, 26.

8 Ch. 41.

9 Ch. 1. The word ch'ang (常), however, may mean lasting, eternal.

bodily senses.[1] It is profound, mysterious, and extremely subtle.[2] Represented as existing eternally, it is in its nature calm, void, solitary, and unchanging;[3] but represented as in operation, it revolves through the universe of being, acting everywhere, but acting "mysteriously, spontaneously, and without effort."[4] It contains matter, and an inherent power of production ; and though itself formless, it yet comprehends all possible forms.[5] It is the ultimate cause of the universe, and it is the model or rule for all creatures, but chiefly for man.[6] It represents also that ideal state of perfection in which all things acted harmoniously and spontaneously, and when good and evil were unknown; and the return to which constitutes the *summum bonum* of existence.[7] Lao-tzŭ speaks of the *Tao* under various metaphors—it is the spirit of the void[8] (lit., spirit of the valley)—a hollow utensil[9]—a river or ocean[1]—a parent[2]—a ruler.[3] We will have more to say of this *Tao* shortly; but the above will perhaps suffice for the present to give an idea of what meaning Lao-tzŭ at-

1 Chs. 14, 35.
2 Ch. 1, &c.
3 Ch. 25.
4 Chs. 25, 37.
5 Chs. 14, 21.
6 Chs. 1, 51.
7 See chs. 18, 38.
8 Ch. 6. The character 谷 is, however, also rendered otherwise in this page. See Yi-yuan's edition and that in the 十子全書.
9 Ch. 4.
1 Ch. 32. 2 Chs. 24, 52.
3 Ch. 51. The *Tao* is also, however, said not to rule over the world. See ch. 34.

tached to the word, or rather, it should be said, the mean-ings; for he does not seem to have had in his mind a very clear conception of what *Tao* actually was.

The next thing we have to do is to endeavour to find a word which will translate *Tao* in this, its transcendental use—a matter of no easy accomplishment. Pauthier, as has been seen, renders it by " *Grande voie* du monde," by "Raison suprême universelle :" he also sometimes speaks of it simply as " Raison"[4] or " Logos." Rémusat[5] also renders it by "Logos" or " Raison ;" and it is by the term "Raison" or "Logos" that English writers translate the character *Tao* when it refers to the peculiar doctrines of Lao-tzŭ and his real or pretended followers. Julien, however, dissents from this interpretation, and rightly I think. After giving an account of *Tao* as taught by the Taoists themselves, he says :—" Il parait donc impossible de le (i.e., *Tao*) prendre pour la *raison primordiale*, pour *l'intelligence sublime* qui a créé et qui régit le monde."[6] It is with great hesitation and reluc-tance, however, that I find myself unable to adopt Julien's own translation—" Voie," or Way. I quite agree with him as to the reason for not adopting the term Reason—namely, that *Tao* as represented by Lao-tzŭ is devoid of thought, judgment, and intelligence (as to action, Lao-tzŭ is appa-rently not quite consistent with himself.) Thus it is quite impossible to make it identical with the *Logos* of Plato, and almost absurd to identify it with the divine *Logos* of the Neoplatonists of Alexandria. But I do not think that the

4 Chine Moderne, p. 851.

5 Mélanges Posthumes, p. 167, and in the Mélanges Asiatiques. See also Julien's Introduction, p. xli.

6 Introduction, p. xiii.

word *way* is the best we can use to translate *Tao*, and this
for several reasons. A way implies a way-maker apart from
and antecedent to it, but *Tao* was before all other existences.
Again, when Lao-tzŭ speaks of it as indeterminate, as profound, and finally as producing, nourishing, and absorbing
the universe, these terms can scarcely be applied to a way,
however metaphorically used. Julien says:—"Le sens de
Voie, que je donne au mot *Tao* 道, résulte clairement des
passages suivants de *Lao-tseu*: 'Si j'etais doué de quelque
prudence, je marcherais dans le grand *Tao*' (dans la grande
Voie).—Le grand *Tao* est très-uni (la grande *Voie* est tres-
unie), mais le peuple aime les sentiers (ch. LIII)." " Le *Tao*
peut être regardé comme la mère de l'univers. Je ne connais
pas son nom ; pour le qualifier, je l'appelle le *Tao* ou la *Voie*
(ch. XXV)."[7] Now in the former of the two cases here
cited the expression *ta tao* 大道 means, I think, the great
course of duty which all men ought to pursue, but especially
those who are in authority—the way of the magistrate or
ruler; an interpretation which seems to be supported by the
rest of the chapter, though some of the commentators seem
to be of the same opinion with Julien.[8] It is to be observed that this scholar translates the words "*ta tao*" by "la
grande Voie," but in the same chapter renders the words "*fei
tao tsai*" 非道哉 simply by "ce n'est point pratiquer le *Tao*."
The chapter from which the latter of the above two passages
is cited by Julien also seems to require another word than
way to translate *Tao*, and the same remark applies to the
occurrence of the word in several other places throughout

7 Introduction, p. xiii.

8 See Wu-ch'ăng's note to the passage.

the *Tao-té Ching.*[9] We may say of the *Tao*, as "Voie" or Way, that it revolves everywhere; but we can scarcely speak of it as being parent of the Universe—the first and highest existence. *Way* or *road* is, no doubt, one of the earliest meanings of the character *Tao*, and that which underlies many of its other uses. Nor is it very difficult to trace its progress from the perfectly concrete *course* or *channel*, and the abstract *line* or *guide*, to the ideal *path* or *course* which universal nature eternally and unchangingly pursues. What Lao-tzŭ does, as it seems to me, is to identify Nature and her ideal course; and as he could find no more general word whereby to express this ultimate ideal unity, hé uses the word *Tao* to designate it, just as a mathematician uses x to express an unknown quantity.

In order to appreciate Lao-tzŭ's system properly, we must substitute for *Tao* a word corresponding as closely as possible to it in width of meaning and vagueness of association. It bears a somewhat close analogy to the *Apeiron* of the old Ionic philosopher Anaximander; but the Indeterminate or the Indefinite is rather an awkward word to be frequently using, and we do not know enough of Anaximander's system to warrant us in substituting the *Apeiron* for *Tao*. In modern times, again, the *Substance* in Spinoza's philosophy, and the *Absolute* in Schelling's, resemble it in many points; but neither could serve as a proper translation. I have accordingly determined to express *Tao* by our word *Nature*, using it in its widest and most abstract sense—"great creating Nature." But I do not wish to be understood as implying that this word corresponds exactly to *Tao*—far from it. I use it simply as in my opinion the nearest approach we can

9 *E. g.*, chs. 16, 14, &c.

get.[1] So, then, we may say of Lao-tzŭ's system that it refers
all matter and spirit in the universe to one original Nature,
from which they both originated, by which they are main-
tained, and into which they are to be finally absorbed. This
is the first general observation I have to make on his philosophy. .

Again, Lao-tzŭ's philosophy is eminently an ethical or
rather a politico-ethical system. All his teachings aim at
making man a better individual, and a better member of
society. Whatever the subject be on which he discourses,
there is generally a moral allusion or a moral lesson taught
in allegory; and the high value which he assigns to moral
excellence above all showy accomplishments deserves our
greatest commendation, even though we dissent from his   .
disparaging view of intellectual acquirements. He appeals
more to the heart than to the mind—more to the Hebraistic
side of our nature than to the Hellenistic (to use Mr. Mat-
thew Arnold's language); and the *Tao-tĕ ching* is more a
book of skeleton sermons than a book of "reasoned truth."
The intellect, indeed, is not only depressed; but is even
sometimes spoken of unfavourably, as opposed to the bene-
ficial operation of Nature (*Tao*) on men's hearts.

Further, the system of Lao-tzŭ is one purely speculative,
and *a priori* (in the Kantian sense). There is in it no
gathering of facts—no questioning of nature—no rising from
particular facts or truths of greater and greater generality.
There is, in short, little or nothing of the spirit of the
inductive philosophy of modern times to be found in the

1 There are several passages in the *Tao-tĕ ching* where Nature could
not be used to translate *Tao*; but this may in some cases arise from the
fact that Lao-tzŭ's conception of Nature was very different from ours.

Tao-tĕ chíng. It "nobly takes the *a priori* road," beginning with the universal cause, and coming down to particular facts; frames hypotheses about nature and morals, and tries to make existing circumstances conform to them. This is the character, however, which it has in common with nearly all early systems of philosophy, and even with some of very modern times. An utterly wrong method we believe it to be; but we can easily forgive it in Lao-tzŭ, when we take into consideration the circumstances amid which he lived, and the nature and amount of the materials at his hand.

The last characteristic of Lao tzŭ's teachings to which I shall allude at present is that they are all imbued with a genial and sympathetic spirit, regarding man not merely as an individual, and not merely as a member of human society, but also a citizen of the universe, if I may use the expression. Modesty, gentleness, forbearance, and self-denial are his constant watchwords. He ever inculcates on man, especially in his highest development, a sympathy not only with his fellow men, but also with all the creatures of the earth, and even with inanimate nature. This doctrine results, no doubt, from the leading idea that all owe their origin to the one all producing, all nourishing nature; and it is a doctrine of which Lao-tzŭ seems to have been very fond. He frequently alludes to it as the duty and advantage of man to be humble, gentle, and never striving; and he utterly abhors the idea of violence, and the ostentation of superiority. He goes to excess, however, I think, in his notions about a peaceful, non-interfering mode of life; and carries his doctrine of the imitation of Nature (*Tao*) to unwarranted lengths.

Having thus described generally the nature of the teachings of the *Tao-tĕ chíng*, I shall now proceed to examine them more in detail. In doing so it will be convenient to consider them under the three leading divisions of Speculative Physics, Politics and Ethics. I must, however, beg pardon of the pale shade of their author for doing so, as I am certain that he would not sanction this division; and at the same time I must forewarn the reader that he is not to think that subjects in his opinion appertaining to these three departments are kept rigorously distinct. Lao-tzŭ, like Plato and some other philosophers, makes Physics and Politics subordinate parts of Ethics—the grand, all embracing study. So, when reading in the *Tao-té ching* about matters which we regard as belonging peculiarly to one or other of these divisions, we must endeavour to regard them from Lao-tzŭ's point of view—viz., as part of one universal, all containing nature. If we leave out the important word which I enclose in brackets, and substitute some such word as *yet* or *still*, we find in the writings of a great English poet of the 18th century sentiments very similar to those of the Chinese sage who lived more than two thousand years before him :—

> " All are but parts of one stupendous whole,
> Whose body nature is, and [God] the soul ;
> That, changed through all, and yet in all the same ;
> Great in the earth, as in the ethereal frame ;
> Warms in the sun, refreshes in the breeze,
> Glows in the stars, and blossoms in the trees,
> Lives through all life, extends through all extent,
> Spreads undivided, operates unspent ;
> Breathes in our soul, informs our mortal part,
> As full, as perfect, in a hair as heart :
> As full, as perfect, in vile man that mourns,
> As the rapt seraph that adores and burns :
> To it no high, no low, no great, no small ;
> It fills, it bounds, connects, and equals all. "

CHAPTER V.

SPECULATIVE PHYSICS.

What was Lao-tzŭ's conception of the Cosmos? To this question we are unfortunately unable to give a clear and satisfactory answer. It is only occasionally, and then usually by way of illustration, that he alludes to the material world or to the physical and mental constitution of man. All that we can do, accordingly, is to examine the miscellaneous passages in which he refers to these subjects, and collect from them what information we can as to the notions which Lao-tzŭ entertained about the origin and nature of the universe; and we must be prepared to find under the head of speculative physics many more matters than ought properly, according to our ideas, to be so included.

The first point to be noticed is that, as has been already seen, Lao-tzŭ refers all existing creatures to an eternal, all-producing, all-sustaining unity, which he calls Nature (Tao). He does not distinguish between mind and matter, nor would he, in my opinion, have recognised any fundamental or generic difference between them. Whether, however, spirit and matter were identical or diametrically opposite, they had a common origin in Tao. But though usually he thus refers all things to nature (Tao) as their first cause, yet

he sometimes seems to speak of the universe as coming from
nothing.[1] Nor is there any contradiction here, since Lao-tzŭ
regarded non-existence (Wu 無) as in certain circumstances identical with existence (Yu 有); the latter being
merely the former contemplated from a different point of
view. This opinion, if not explicitly stated by himself, is
at least implied in his writings, and is explicitly stated by
one of his disciples.[2] It must be mentioned, however, that
Chu-hsi (朱熹) ascribes the very opposite doctrine to
Lao-tzŭ, who, he says, regarded existence and non-existence
as two, whereas Chou-tzŭ (周子) regarded them as one.[3]
In the Tao-tê Ching the originator of the universe is referred
to under the names Non-Existence, Existence, Nature (Tao)
and various other designations—all which, however, represent one idea in various manifestations. It is in all cases
Nature (Tao) which is meant, and we are now prepared to
examine the part which Lao-tzŭ assigns to this Tao in the
production and regulation of the physical world.

Tao, as spoken of by Lao-tzŭ, may be considered as a
potential or as an actual existence, and under this latter head
it may be contemplated in itself and as an operating agent
in the universe. Regarded as a potential existence it may,
when compared with actual existence, be pronounced non-
existence. It is from this point of view imperceptible to
man, and can be spoken of only negatively; and so such
terms as non-existence (無), the unlimited or infinite (無
極), the non-exerting (無爲), the matterless (無物),

1 See Ch. 40.
2 See Preface to Tao-tê-ching-chie 道德經解.
3 See note in the T'ai-chi-t'u-shuo (太極圖說). Hsing-li-ta-
ch'uan. Vol. I.

are the expressions used with reference to Tao thus considered.[4] Accordingly Lao-tzŭ, when speaking of it as a potential existence, as the logical antecedent of all perceptible existence—seems to regard it as equivalent to the primeval Nothing or Chaos. So too the Yuan-miao-nei-p'ien (元妙 內篇) says that the great Tao which arose in non-exertion is the ancestor of all things.[5] From this state, however, it passes into the condition of actual existence, a transition which is expressed under the metaphor of generation.[6] To this doctrine, that existence is generated from non-existence, Chu-hsi objects; but his objection arises chiefly, I think, from supposing that Lao-tzŭ regarded them as two distinct things, whereas his doctrine on this subject is exactly like that of Chou-tzŭ, with which Chu-hsi seems to agree.[7] We are not to suppose that Nature is ever simply and entirely potential to the utter exclusion of actuality, or vice versâ: on the contrary, these two existences or conditions are represented as alternately generating each the other.[8] Thus the potential (or nominal non-existence) may be supposed to be in time later than the actual, though the latter must always be logically regarded as consequent on the former. In itself, again, Tao, regarded as an actual existence is, as has been seen, calm, void, eternal, unchanging and bare of all qualities. Regarded as an agent operating throughout the

4 See Ch. 28, 46.

5 Yuan-chien, &c., p. 818.

6 Ch. 40. Compare with this Aristotle's statement, "Nature spoken of as generation is the path to Nature." See Essay V. in Grant's Aristotle's Ethics, vol. 1.

7 See his 全書, Ch. 85.

8 Ch. 2.

universe, on the other hand, *Tao* may be spoken of as great, changing, far-extending, and finally returning (to the state of potentiality).[9] A late author gives a curious illustration of the above notions of Lao-tzŭ, taken from the well-known habits of the Ateuchus with reference to the propagation of its species, but this author proceeds on the supposition that non-existence and existence are different. We have now to combine these two conceptions of Tao, as a potential and as an actual existence. Though void, shapeless, and immaterial, it yet contains the potentiality of all substance and shape, and from itself it produces the universe,[1] diffusing itself over or permeating all space. It is said to have generated the world,[2] and is frequently spoken of as the mother of this latter[3]—"the dark primeval mother, teeming with dreamy beings." All things that exist submit to Tao as their chief, but it displays no lordship over them.[4] In the spring time it quickens the dead world, clothes it as with a garment, and nourishes it, yet the world knows not its fostermother. A distinction, however, is made—the nameless is said to be the origin of heaven and earth, while the named is the mother of the myriad objects which inhabit the earth. Though there is nothing done in the universe which is not done by Nature, though all things depend on it for their existence, yet in no case is Nature seen acting.[5] It is in its own deep self an unit—the smallest possible quantity—yet it

9 Ch. 25, see Panthier, Chine Moderne, p. 359.
1 See Chs. 21, 25, compare Emerson Miscellanies, p. 32.
2 Ch. 51.
3 Chs. 6, 52.
4 Ch. 34.
5 See Chs. 37, 41, 43.

prevails over the wide expanse of the universe, operating unspent but unseen.[6]

We now come to the generations of the heavens and the earth, and their history is thus given by Lao-tzŭ.[7] Tao generated One, One generated Two, Two generated Three, and Three generated the material world. That is, according to the explanation given by some, Nature (Tao) generated the Yin-ch'i (陰氣), the passive and inferior element in the composition of things; this in its turn produced the Yang-ch'i (陽氣), the active and superior element; which again produced Ho (和), that is, that harmonious agreement of the passive and active elements which brought about the production of all things.[8] Another explanation is that Tao considered as Non-existence produced the Great Extreme (T'ai-chi 太極), which produced the passive and active elements; then Harmony united these two and generated the universe.[9] Of this section of the Tao-tê Ching Rémusat observes—"En effet, Lao-tseu explique, d'une manière qui est entièrement conforme à la doctrine Platonicienne, comment les deux principes, celui du ciel et celui de la terre, ou l'air grossier et l'ether, sont liés entre eux par un *Souffle* qui les unit et qui produit *l'harmonie*. Il est impossible d'exprimer plus clairement les idées de Timée de Locres, dont les termes semblent la traduction du passage Chinois."[1] The doctrines, however, on the formation of the world put into the

6 See Chs. 82, 89.

7 Ch. 42.

8 See Wu-ch'êng's note to the passage.

9 See the note on this passage in the Tao-tê-ching-chie; compare also the peculiar interpretation given by Ta-chün.

1 Mémoire, &c., p. 86.

mouth of Timæus, and the ideas of Lao-tzŭ on this subject, seem to me to have very little in common. The Greek philosopher makes a personal deity the artificer of the universe, fashioning the world out of the bright and solid elements, fire and earth, which he unites by means of air and water, thus forming a friendship and harmony indissoluble by any except the author. The *harmony* of Lao-tzŭ, on the other hand is, if we understand him aright, only the uncon-flicting alternation of the two cosmical elements, and there is no divine Demiurg in his system. There is, however, a statement in the Timæus which resembles Lao-tzŭ's statement on this subject, and to which we will refer hereafter.

First in order after Tao is Tien (天), or the material heaven above us. This is represented as pure and clear in consequence of having obtained the One—that is, in conse-quence of having participated in the great "over-soul" or Universal Nature.[2] Were heaven to lose its purity and clearness it would be in danger of destruction. Of the heavenly bodies and their revolutions, Lao-tzŭ does not make mention, nor have we any means of ascertaining what were his ideas respecting them. Nearly all that he says about Tien or heaven is metaphorical, with apparent refer-ence to an agent endowed with consciousness (according to our ways of thinking). Thus he speaks of it as enduring for a long period because it does not exist for itself; as being free from partiality towards any of the creatures in the world; as being next in dignity above a king and below Tao, and as taking this last for its rule of conduct.[3]

The space between heaven and earth is represented as

2 See Cha. 16, 39.
3 See Chs. 7, 5, 16, 25.

like a bottomless bag or tube,[4] though this is perhaps
merely a metaphorical expression. The earth itself is at
rest,[5] this being the specific nature which it has as the result
of its participation in Tao. The heavens are always revol-
ving over the earth, producing the varieties of the seasons,
vivifying, nourishing, and killing all things; but it remains
stationary in calm repose. Were it to lose the informing
nature which makes it so, the earth would probably be set
in motion. Its place is next in order after heaven which
it takes as its model. It is impartial, spontaneous, unostentatious, and exists long because it does not exist for itself.
Neither in heaven nor on earth can anything violent endure
for a lengthened period. The whirlwind and heavy rains
may come, but they do not last even for a day.[6]

Next to heaven and earth are the "myriad things," that
is, the animate and inanimate objects which surround us;
and here again it must be borne in mind that Lao-tzŭ's
allusions to these matters are only incidental and by way of
illustration generally. As has been seen, all things spring
from and participate in Nature, which is, as it were, their
mother. This Nature (Tao) is, as we have seen, imperceptible
in itself, and when considered merely as a potentiality; but
it bodies itself forth and takes a local habitation and a name
in all the objects which exist in the universe, and thus it
becomes palpable to human observation—not in its essence
but only in its workings. Now this manifestation of Nature

---

4 See Ch. 5; Julien, however, translates the passage, " L'être qui
est entre le ciel et la terre ressemble à un soufflet de forge, &c.

5 Ch. 39.

6 Ch. 23.

constitutes for each object or class of objects in the world its Tě (德)—that is, what it has received or obtained from Tao, according to some commentators. Tě is usually translated by *virtus*, but this word very inadequately represents the meaning of the word in this connection. Sometimes it seems to be almost synonymous with Tao, and has functions assigned to it which at other times are represented as pertaining to this latter. If, however, we regard Tao as the great or universal Nature, we may consider Tě as the particular Nature with which creatures are endowed out of the former. It is also the conscious excellence which man and all other creatures obtain when spontaneity is lost. Thus Lao-tzŭ regards all things as equally with man under the care of Nature, which produces and nourishes all alike. Heaven and earth, he says, have no partialities—they regard the " myriad things " as the straw-made dogs which were formed for the sacrifices and prayers for rain, and cast aside when the rites were finished.[7] In another passage of the Tao-tě Ching it is said that Tao generates all things, Tě nourishes all things, Matter (Wu 物) bodies them forth, and Order (勢) gives them perfection.[8]

Lao-tzŭ, in accordance with popular Chinese ideas, speaks of five colours, five sounds, and five tastes;[9] and he attributes to these a baneful influence on man, whom he teaches to overcome and nullify them as much as possible. All things in the world, moreover, are arranged in a system of dualism.[1]

7 Ch. 5.
8 Ch. 51; but see the different interpretation given by Julien.
9 Ch. 12.
1 See Chs. 2, 11, 29, 36. Compare Emerson's Essay on Compensation—*Essays*, vol. I.

Motion is always followed by rest, and this again by motion.
Long and short, high and low, mutually succeed each other,
and are merely relative terms. Solidity gives the object,
and hollowness gives its utility, as in the case of wooden or
earthen vessels. When a thing is to be weakened it must
first have been strengthened ; to that from which there is to
be taken there must first have been given. This dualism
will be seen to extend into other regions besides the physical
world, and it is needless to refer to it at greater length at
present.

Further, Lao-tzŭ seems to have regarded all existing
things as having a set time during which to endure. Nature
engenders them, nourishes them and finally receives them
back into its bosom. They flourish until they attain to the
state of completeness, which is soon lost, and then decay and
final dissolution ensue.[2] The tree grows from the tiny
sapling to its full maturity, then decays and returns to dark
Mother Nature. The process as conceived and sketched by
the ancient sage is beautifully described in the words of
Tennyson—

> " Lo ! in the middle of the wood,
>   The folded leaf is woo'd from out the bud
>   With winds upon the branch, and there
>   Grows green and broad and takes no care,
>   Sun-steep'd at noon, and in the moon
>   Nightly dew-fed ; and turning yellow
>   Falls, and floats adown the air.

2 See Chs. 10, 55.

Lo! sweeten'd with the summer light
The full-juiced apple, waxing over-mellow,
Drops in a silent autumn night.
All its allotted length of days,
The flower ripens in its place,
Ripens and fades, and falls, and hath no toil,
Fast-rooted in the fruitful soil."[3]

Lao-tzŭ's mode of contemplating natural phenomena is,
indeed, altogether much more like that of the poetical
metaphysician than that of the physicist. He does not look
upon a stream, for example, as composed of certain chemical
elements in certain proportions, as running at a calculable
rapid rate, carrying with it an alarming amount of mud, and
having in each microscopic drop exactly so many thousands
of animalcule. He thinks of it rather as at first a tiny
stream up among the hills, scooping out the hard earth, and
slowly wearing away impeding stones, in order to make a
channel for its waters; as flowing thence down into the vale
where it gives itself up to enrich the fields; then as passing
on thence to join the brimming river, and finally submit
itself to the great sea.[4] He regards everything from an
ethical point of view, and finds a lesson everywhere. He
does not regard the study of nature as consisting in the
investigation of colour, sound, heat, and such things—the
less one has to do with these the better. The study should
be carried on in one's own room without any adventitious
aids. The student must overcome his affections and passions

3 *The Lotos Eaters.*
4 See Chs. 8, 78.

before he can attain to a knowledge of the great mysteries
of Nature, but having once attained the serene heights of
desireless existence he can know all things.[5] This is no-
doubt a bad way of studying nature, and one which would
never conduct to the material benefit of humanity. Yet it
also has its uses. It helps to make us " mingle with the universe," have a lower appreciation of ourselves, and sympathise
affectionately with all that surrounds us. We have abundance of room in the world for the two classes of philosophers
—those who experiment on Nature with a view to the material progress of mankind, and those who regard her with the
dutiful love of a son for a mother.

In the teachings of Lao-tzŭ in Speculative Physics, as
sketched above, the student of philosophy will find many
ideas resembling others with which he is already more familiar. To those of the sages of Ancient Greece it is perhaps
unnecessary for me to do more than refer. With them as
living also in the comparative childhood of the world Lao-tzŭ
might naturally be supposed to have considerable affinity.
In the Timæus of Plato there is a passage which does not
accord with the rest of that work, nor with the spirit of the
other Platonic dialogues, and which bears considerable
resemblance to the doctrine of Lao-tzŭ about the primordial
all-producing Nature (Tao). The hero of the dialogue, if
such an expression may be used, Timæus himself, suddenly
leaves the train of imaginative discourse which he had been
for some time pursuing about the visible universe and the
mode in which the divine artificer constructed it, and he
introduces a new conception, that of the primeval mother,

5 See Chs. 1, 47.

formless, immortal, and indestructible.[6] Reference has already been made to the resemblance between Lao-tzŭ's teachings and those of Anaximander, and Hegel says of the latter's notion, that the ἄπειρον is the principle from which endless worlds or gods originate and into which they vanish, that it sounds quite Oriental.[7] But not only are Lao-tzŭ's speculations on physics like those of other ancients, they resemble also those of many modern philosophers, and his theory about the study of Nature may well be compared with that of Schelling. The Tao Itself, or the primordial existence, appears under various names in the history of Philosophy. It is the Tai-chi (太極) or Great Extreme—the Tai-yi (太一) or Great Unit—the *Anima Mundi*—the Absolute —the Vital Force—Gravity—Caloric—when considered as universally active and productive.

> "There is but one vast universal dynamic, one mover, one might,
> Variously operant under the various conditions it finds;
> And we call that by turns electricity, friction, caloric, and light,
> Which is none of these things, and yet all of them. Ask of the waves
>   and the winds,
> Ask of the stars of the firmament, ask of the flowers of the field;
> They will answer you all of them, naming it each by a different name.
> For the meaning of Nature is neither wholly conceal'd nor reveal'd ;
> But her mind is seen to be single in her acts that are nowhere the
>   same."[8]

6 *Timæus*, cb. xviii. (Ed. Stallbaum). See also Grote's Plato, Vol. III., p. 266-7. *Timæus*, however, introduces reason and other ideas not consonant with Lao-tzŭ's teachings.

7 *Geschichte, &c.*, vol. i, p. 204.

8 Robert Lytton's—"The Man of Science."

Further, Lao-tzŭ represents pure or abstract existence as
identical with non-existence, and in our own century Hegel
has said that Being and Non-being are the same.[9]   Again,
Lao-tzŭ speaks of the ultimate existence as that out of which
all other existences have proceeded, and he regards it as becoming active and producing from having been inactive
and quiescent.   So many modern philosophers have main-
tained that God made all things out of himself; and in
the opinion of some the Deity became personal from
being impersonal, and the Infinite manifested itself as finite
in the created universe.[1]   But the great point on which
Lao-tzŭ differs from the large majority of modern thinkers
with regard to the First Cause is that he never introduces or
supposes the element of personality; consequently will and
design are excluded from his conception of the primordial
existence.[2]   Here, I think, he is logically more correct than
the modern philosopher referred to above, although his
notions may be much farther from the actual truth than
theirs.   Again, when Lao-tzŭ speaks of Nature (Tao) as the
source whence all things spring—as that which informs and
cherishes all the world—and as that into which all living
creatures, high and low, finally return—he says what many
others have expressed in terms often very similar.   I select

9 See Lewes' History of Philosophy, vol. ii., p. 533 (New Edition).

1 On this subject information will be found in E. Laisset's Precurseurs
et Disciples de Descartes, p. 210, &c.; Hamilton's Discussions; Lewis'
History of Philosophy, vol. ii.

2 Fichte (the elder), however, is at one with Lao-tzŭ on this
point.

only two or three instances by way of illustration. The Pythagorean doctrine is thus put by Virgil—

—"deum (i.e. animum) ire per omnes
Terrasque tractusque maris cœlumque profundum ;
Hinc pecudes, armenta, viros, genus omne ferarum,
Quemque sibi tenues nascentem arcessere vitas ;
Scilicet huc reddi deinde ac resoluta referri
Omnia."[3]

Strikingly similar to Lao-tzŭ's words are those of the Preacher—"For that which befalleth the sons of men befalleth beasts; even one thing befalleth them; as the one dieth, so dieth the other; yea, they have all one breath; so that a man hath no pre-eminence above a beast; for all is vanity. All go unto one place; all are of the dust, and all turn to dust again."[4] In later times Coleridge has said— "Life is the one universal soul, which by virtue of the enlivening Breath, and the informing word, all organised bodies have in common, each after its kind. This, therefore, all animals possess, and man as an animal."[5] More closely resembling Lao-tzŭ's statements on this subject, however, are the words of Dr. Büchner—"D'un autre côté n'oublions pas non plus, que nous ne sommes qu' une partie imperceptible, quoique nécessaire, du grand tout qui constitue le monde et que nous devons tôt ou tard perdu notu personalité

---

3 Georgica, Bk. iv., vv. 221-6. The rest of the passage does not apply. Compare also Cicero's criticism on the Pythagorean doctrine, in the De Nat. Deorum, ch 1, § 11.

4 Eccles, Ch. III., vv. 19 and 20.

5 Aids to Reflection, p. 4.

pour rentrer dans la masse commune. La Matière dans
son ensemble est la mère d'ou tout provient et ou tout
retourne."[6]

As we proceed we will find other doctrines of our author
resembling those of writers and thinkers far removed from
him in time and space. The illustrations given and referred
to above will suffice to show that, in speculations about
Nature and the great mystery of existence, we are little, if
anything, superior to "the ancients." The course of speculative philosophy seems to be circular—the same truths and
errors appearing again and again, so that as Coleridge has
said, "For many, very many centuries it has been difficult
to advance a new truth, or even a new error, in the philosophy of the intellect or morals,"[7] or, he might have added,
of theoretical physics. Is it true, after all, that the spirit
of the long-deceased philosopher returns from the Elysian
fields, forgetting by its Lethean draught all the truths and
realities of the eternal, ever-the-same world, to inform again
a human body? We know that Malebranche's character was
like that of Plato. Schelling, even in external appearance,
resembled Socrates; Hegel is called the modern Proclus;
and the soul of Lao-tzŭ may have transmigrated into Emerson. This last has been chained to "a weight of nerves,"
and located in circumstances altogether unlike those of its
former earthly existence, a fact which would account for
many points of unlikeness. The informing spirit, however,
has known no change in "its own deep self:"

6 Force et Matière, p. 93 (French translation).

7 Biographia Lita., ch. 5; compare also the remarkable words of Hegel.
Geschichte, &c., Vol. i., p. 148.

LAO-TZŬ.

" Our birth is but a sleep and a forgetting :
    The soul that rises with us, our life's star,
Hath had elsewhere its setting,
    And cometh from afar ;
Not in entire forgetfulness
And not in utter nakedness,
But trailing clouds of glory do we come
From God, who is our home."

CHAPTER VI.

POLITICS.

We now breathe a freer air—escaped from the trammels of Physics, and at large in the wide spaces of Politics. Here Lao-tzŭ speaks more plainly and fully, and it is easily seen that he is dealing with congenial subjects. To us also his political aphorisms will come with more freshness and delight than the speculations about things much more beyond his ken with which we were last engaged. Yet we must not expect to find in the *Tao-tĕ Ching* a treatise on Politics, or a discourse on the best form of government. Lao-tzŭ does not present to us a wax figment of his own imagination—an ideal republic, an Utopia, or a New Atlantis. He looks to his own country as it was then, oppressed and miserable, and he endeavours to recall those in authority to a noble and generous mode of government. His standard of political excellence may be ideal, and some of his maxims may be fanciful, and even bad; still we will find in all a genial human philosophy, which even we of the enlightened nineteenth century cannot utterly despise.

"Politics," says Sir G. C. Lewes, "relate to human action so far as it concerns the public interest of a community, and is not merely private or ethical. Human action, thus defined, consists of—1, the acts and relations of a sovereign government, both with respect to its own subjects and other sovereign governments; 2, the acts and relations of members of the political community, so far as they concern the government, or the community at large, or a considerable portion of it."[1] Lao-tzŭ's teachings in politics refer more to the former than to the latter of these two divisions. He does not, however, omit to notice the relations of the different members of the state, as well to the government as to each other; but he relegates this subject to the province of ethics. He considers the people more in their private relations than as bound by legal ties to the performance of certain acts, and the abstaining from certain other acts, towards their fellows. Nor is it from the political stand-point that he contemplates the nature and distribution of wealth, a subject which properly belongs to politics. These and similar matters are all assigned to the private relations of man to the Universal Nature, and so they will come more properly under the head of ethics.

Having premised thus much, I now proceed to set forth Lao-tzŭ's teachings about " the acts and relations of a sovereign government, both with respect to its own subjects and other sovereign governments; " and

1. *Of the institution of the Sovereign.*—It is to the people that he assigns the original appointment of an emperor, and he gives a peculiar reason for the institution. A bad man still has the law of Nature (*Tao*) in him; and he is not to be cast aside as a hopeless case, seeing he may be transformed into a virtuous man. Accordingly emperors and

1 Treatise on the Methods of Observation. Reasoning in Politics, vol. 1, p. 44.

magistrates were appointed, whose duty it was to save, as it
were, by precept and example, those who had gone astray.[2]
Thus Lao-tzŭ's idea of the sovereign is so far purely ethical.
He does not conceive of him so much as the judge and ruler
of the people as their model and instructor. The man whom
the people elect, however, is also the elected of Heaven.[3]
As in the case of Saul the Israelites anointed him whom
the Lord had chosen, so the people raise to the throne him
whom Heaven has appointed. Princes exercise government,
because they have received that destiny as their share of
the Universal Nature.[4] They obtain their *One*—their indi-
vidualizing nature—in order that they may rule righteously.
Sometimes he seems to use the term *Shêng-jên* (聖人) as
synonymous with *Wang* (王), or King.[5] Now the *Shêng-jên*
is the man who by his nature is completely virtuous, perfectly in harmony with the ways heaven has ordained. He is
in short the stoic *Sapiens*, and whether he actually administer
public affairs or not, is still a king. The term *Saint*, by
which Julien renders this expression, scarcely conveys its
full meaning; as the *Shêng-jên* is not only holy, but also
supremely wise. He is the ideal or typical man, who rules
over and transforms the world; and, failing a better, I shall
translate it by the expression *godlike man*. In ancient times,
it was the *Shêng-jên*, or godlike man, who was appointed
ruler; and if such were the case now, the world would be
in peace and prosperity. The man who is destined to

2 See Ch. 62. In Pi-yuan's edition, 天下 is the reading, instead
of 天子 of the ordinary texts.

3 See Wu-ch'êng's note to ch. 62 (52 in his edition).

4 Ch. 39.

5 See Chs. 3, 5. Compare Emerson (Essays, Vol. 2, pp. 208-9).

become king will not use violence to obtain the honour.[6] On the contrary he will be humble and yielding; and so, as water wears away the hard opposing rocks, he will finally triumph. In confirmation hereof Lao-tzŭ cites the saying of a godlike man:—"To bear the reproaches of a kingdom is to preside over the sacrifices to the gods of the land and grain (i.e. to be prince), and to bear a kingdom's misfortunes is to be king of the whole empire"—words true, though seeming paradoxical.[7] Lao-tzŭ, however, has a very high opinion of the position and dignity of the sovereign. There are four great things in the universe, and he is one of them; the remaining three being Nature (Tao), Heaven, and Earth.[8] In another place he even puts the king immediately before Heaven.[9]

2. The relations of the ruler to his subjects.—With Lao-tzŭ, as with all Chinese writers on politics, the mode in which government ought to be conducted is a supremely important subject. In his homely manner, he compares the ruling of a large kingdom to the cooking of a small fish, or the handling of a fine and delicate implement.[1] Too much cooking spoils the implement. So is it with the kingdom. It is an etherial instrument which cannot be wrought with—if one works with it he destroys it, and if one handles it he loses it.

The first duty of the ruler is to rectify himself—to over-

6 Ch 29.

7 Ch. 78.

8 Ch. 25. We must remember that this passage is susceptible of a metaphorical meaning. See Tao tĕ-lsing-ming-chiĕn-hsü.

9 Ch. 16.

1 Chs 60, 29, 64.

come his appetites and passions.[2] He must cultivate virtue
in himself, and proceeding thence he will have it cultivated
in his family, and finally in all the empire; and thus the
kingdom will remain established in his family for generations
to come.[3] He must be serious and grave[4] in his deportment,
remembering the greatness of his charge, and whence it was
derived. By levity of conduct he will lose his ministers,
and by violent proceedings he will lose his throne. His
models ought to be the Earth,[5] which is always in peaceful
rest, and the rulers of antiquity, who followed Nature *(Tao)*.
In the early days of innocence and simplicity, subjects only
knew that they had rulers, so lightly lay the hand of
government on them.[6] Then came the time when rulers
were loved and lauded, then the time when they were
feared, and lastly that in which they were treated with
contumely. The prince of the present time ought to return
as far as possible to the primitive ways. He should, like
the great Universal Nature, be free from show of action[7]—
if he could only keep the law of Nature, his kingdom
would, as a matter of course, be in a state of order
and tranquillity—all things would submit to him, and
become, of their own accord, transformed to a state of good-

2 Chs. 57, 13.

3 Ch. 54.

4 Ch. 26.   For 臣, Ministers, another reading is 平 —that is, the
gravity which brings esteem.

5 Ch. 25.   For 王 here some editions have 人 man.

6 Ch. 17.   This chapter, however, is susceptible of a totally different
interpretation, 太上 being regarded as meaning the highest authority.
For 下 also some read 不, not.

7 Ch. 18.

ness [8]—even the demons would cease to possess elfish power;
or if they still possessed it, they would not use it to the
detriment of men. The prince ought also, at least outward-
ly, to be humble and modest, not arrogating precedence and
superiority, but rather using the language of self-abasement. [9]

In the exercise of government Lao-tzŭ does not allow the
use of violence, and he inveighs nobly against military
oppression. If the prince keep himself from being absorbed
in worldly interests—do not confer honour and emoluments
on brilliant parts—nor prize what the world holds valuable
—nor make display of that which is coveted: his example
will have such virtue that all his subjects will cease from
strife and violence, and live in peaceful obedience. [1] But if
he try to have the empire through force, he will fail. He
who according to the Law of Nature (Tao) would assist the
prince will not compel the empire by arms—this sort of
thing is wont to have its recompense. Where the General
pitches his tent, thorns and briers spring up; and in the
wake of a great army there are inevitably bad years. If
there be necessity for fighting—and only then—he who is
wise in ruling will strike a decisive blow at the fit time,
and then lay down his arms, not glorying in his conquest.
Fine arms are inauspicious implements, hated by all things;
and he who holds to Nature will not continue to use them.
The noble man (君子) in private life esteems the left side,
and in time of war esteems the right—the left being symbo-
lic of the Yang (陽) or preserving principle, and the right
of the Yin (陰) or killing principle. Arms are inauspicious

8 Cha. 37, 82.
9 Cha. 66, 68, 39.
1 Ch. 2.

implements—not such as the noble man employs; he uses
them only when he has no alternative, but he looks on
superiority with indifference, and takes no glory in victory.
He who glories in victory delights in the massacre of men,
and such an one cannot have his will in the empire. To him
who slays a multitude of men, a position of dignity is assigned
corresponding to that of the chief mourner at a funeral, viz.,
the right hand side, which in inauspicious matters is the post
of honour, just as in auspicious matters the left hand side is
the post of honour.[2] Thus not only is the ruler not to use
military power to keep his subjects in subjection, but he is
also not to drag these latter into war for his own aggrandise-
ment. The fighting to which Lao-tzŭ mainly alludes is that
of the different principalities of the country among themselves, and on this subject the words of Pascal may be not
unaptly added to those of our author:—"Le plus grand des
maux est les guerres civiles. Elles sont sûres si on veut
récompenser le merite; car tous diraient qu'ils meritent.
Le mal à craindre d'un sot qui succède par droit de naissance
n'est ni si grand ni si sûr."[3] War is the result, according to
Lao-tzŭ, of bad government, of the lust of power and pro-
perty. If good government prevail in a country, its fleet
horses will be employed on the farm; but if ill government
prevail, and lust and ambition have scope, feuds will continue until war steeds beget war steeds on the plains of the
frontier.[4] Whether, therefore, for the purpose of solidifying
the prince's power over his subjects, or for state aggrandise-
ment, war and all violent measures are interdicted.

2 Chs. 30, 31.

3 Pensées, Art. VII.

4 Ch. 46.

But not only does Lao-tzŭ thus advise the ruler against
using military power in his realm; he also recommends the
doing away with capital punishment—indeed with all punishment whatever. The people do not fear death, and how then
is it to be used to keep them in dread? If the people could
be made to have a constant fear of death, and some commit
a crime, and be apprehended and put to death, would any
one continue to venture on offending? It is presumptuous
then for the magistrate to use capital punishment. There
is the eternal executioner, and he who puts to death
for him is like the man who fells a tree for the head
wood-man; and such an one seldom fails to wound his
hand.[5] Capital punishment is thus reserved for something
superhuman to execute; and the earthly magistrate has
only to endeavour to lead a life free from the appearance of
lust and violence.[6]'

It is by justice that a kingdom is well governed, as by
stratagem a war is conducted.[7] Yet the prince must be
lenient to his people. If restrictions on liberty of action be
multiplied, so that his subjects cannot lift a hand or move
a foot without incurring guilt, they will be prevented from
pursuing their industry, and so become poor.[8]

The levying of excessive taxes[9] by those in authority for
the indulgence of their sensual appetites, also impoverishes
a people, and accordingly in government there is nothing

5 Ch. 74.
6 Ch. 57.
7 Chs. 57, 8.
8 Do. Compare Hobbes (Vol. 2, pp. 178-9, Molesworth Ed.).
9 Ch. 75.

like economy.[1] To keep the court in affluence while the fields are weedgrown and the public granaries exhausted; for the rulers to have expensive clothing, sharp swords, sumptuous food and excessive wealth, is to glory in plunder, but not to follow Nature. Nor may the prince break his word with subjects—as want of faith in him is followed by want of faith in them.[2]

It is not necessary for the ruler to explain the nature and method of his government. On the contrary he ought to keep his counsels and his conduct secret. Inasmuch as the fish cannot with impunity leave its element, so the sharp engines of government may not be displayed.[3] When the laws are numerous and obtrusively exhibited, the people become thieves and robbers; but when they are not so, the people continue decent and orderly.[4] Thus it is better that the rulers keep the populace in a state of ignorance and stupidity.[5] The ancient kings went on this principle, and had peaceful reigns.[6] In his own time Lao-tzŭ considered that the difficulty of keeping the people well governed arose from their being too knowing. He would accordingly like to see them recalled to the ways of primitive simplicity, so that their arms would be unworn, and their boats and cars unused. He would like to have the people return to the manners of the times when knotted cords were still the symbols of words; and would have them relish their food,

1 Chs. 59, 53.
2 Ch. 17.
3 Chs. 86, 58.
4 Ch. 57.
5 Chs. 10, 19.
6 Chs. 65, 3.

enjoy their clothes, feel comfortable in their homes, and delight in their social institutions.[7] He would have them brought to think seriously of death, so that they would end their days in their own country and never leave it for another, even though it were so near that the respective inhabitants could hear the cackling of the fowls and the barking of the dogs in the two places. Thus, while the prince keeps his subjects simple and ignorant, he must have their bodily wants supplied. The godlike man when he rules empties the minds of the people, and fills their stomachs; weakens their wills, and strengthens their bones (that is, their animal power).[8] He treats them as children, and is always kind, postponing his own comfort to their good.

The mode in which the ruler is to obtain respect and esteem from his subjects is by deporting himself humbly towards them, and he must never arrogate greatness to himself.[9] His conduct should be calm and unostentatious, while inwardly he is anxious; and his gravity and quietness of deportment ought never to be departed from. The prince is to save his people, as it were, by setting before them an example of humility, forbearance, and all the other virtues which save a country from being imbroiled in wars and rebellions—he is to be of one heart and one mind with them, and have no will independent of theirs.[1]

7 Ch. 80.

8 Ch. 3. Wu-ch'ĕng's note. Julien, however, translates "Il vide son cœur, &c." Both translations are in harmony with the other teachings of Lao-tzŭ.

9 Chs. 39, 42.

1 Ch. 49.

These are the principal duties of the king to his people as
indicated or conceived of by Lao-tzŭ—the king being in his
contemplation an absolute sovereign. I shall now add, as a
comment, the views on this subject set forth by two other
authors in widely different circumstances. The writer of
Deuteronomy says :—"When thou art come into the land
which the Lord thy God giveth thee, and shalt possess it,
and shalt dwell therein, and shalt say, I will set a king over
me, like as all the nations that *are* about me ; thou shalt in
any wise set *him* king over thee, whom the Lord thy God
shall choose; *one* from among thy brethren shalt thou set
king over thee; thou mayest not set a stranger over thee,
which *is* not thy brother. But he shall not multiply horses
to himself, nor cause the people to return to Egypt, to the
end that he should multiply horses : * * * Neither shall he
multiply wives to himself, that his heart turn not away,
neither shall he greatly multiply to himself silver and gold,
&c. * * * That his heart be not lifted up above his brethren,
and that he turn not aside from the commandment *to* the
right hand or *to* the left; to the end that he may prolong
his days in his kingdom, he, and his children, in the midst
of Israel."[2]

The other writer is the philosopher of Malmesbury. After
establishing for the king a title as extravagantly high as any
oriental flatterer could have done, he proceeds to prescribe
his duties to his people. These are summed up in the
sentence, "The safety of the people is the supreme law "—
according to the old maxim, "Salus populi suprema lex."
Under this are included both spiritual and temporal benefits ;
but the difficulty about the former is left in suspense. Of

2 Ch. xvii., vs. 14 to 20.

the latter he says:—"The benefits of subjects respecting
this life only, may be distributed into four kinds—1, That
they be defended against foreign enemies; 2, That peace be
preserved at home; 3, That they be enriched, as much as
may consist with public security; 4, That they enjoy a
harmless liberty."[3]

3. The next point to be considered is *the relation of a
government to the neighbouring states.* On this subject Lao-
tzŭ has very little to say, and what he does say concerns
only the small feudal dependencies of the kingdom of *Chow.*
All the world—that is, all the world known—was the king's;
but holding under him, at this time indeed only nominally
for the most part, were chiefs of smaller and larger provinces
and principalities. It is of this, in their relations to each
other and to their titular superior, that Lao-tzŭ makes
mention.

The different states in their mutual intercourse ought to
be guided by courtesy and forbearance. The great kingdom
is the reservoir of the small principalities,[4] and ought to
remain in dignified peace, while these come to give in their
allegiance, as the little streams from the mountains flow to
the placid lake or smoothly-flowing river as their king. The
large state ought thus to remain lowly and humble towards
the small one, and not act towards it in an arrogant or
violent manner. When a large kingdom abases itself to a
small principality, and when a small state abases itself to a
large one, it obtains service (and protection) under that large

3 Hobbes' Works, (Molesworth's edition), English, Vol. 2, p. 169.
Compare also Bacon's Essay on Seditions and Troubles (Works, Vol. 6,
p. 408, &c. Ellis and Spedding's Ed.).
4 Cha. 61, 66.

one. It is for this purpose that the small state submits;
and the large kingdom annexes the small states for the purpose of uniting and maintaining the people.

It is fit that the large state should always act humbly and
meekly, and that the small states should own its supremacy;
there will thus be no need of fighting. There is no greater
misfortune in the world than to take up a quarrel on a slight
pretext.[3] As the soldiers say, it is much better to bear
than to make the attack—to yield considerably than to
advance a little. That is, it is better to have one's own
territory invaded than to make aggression on that of another.
The king who is yielding and compliant is sure to be ulti-
mately victorious. If, however, a prince must go to war,
whether to defend his own dominions, or at the bidding of
his sovereign, he must show clemency. It is the tender
hearted who gains the victory in the pitched battle, and who
succeeds in keeping the beleaguered city.

By words like these the philosopher endeavoured to
dissuade the princes and barons of his time from the border
warfare in which they were perpetually engaged. The
mutual aggressions and reprisals of these chiefs were in his
days desolating the kingdom and gradually reducing it to
the condition favourable to the production of a tyrant. A
few centuries after Lao-tzŭ's death the man arose who made
himself king over all the empire (王天下), but he was
very unlike the king depicted by Lao-tzŭ and Confucius
and Mencius.

4. On the latter of the two departments into which Sir
G. C. Lewes divides Politics, namely, the relations of the
subjects to their ruler and to each other, Lao-tzŭ, as I have

5 Ch. 69.

already intimated, does not dilate. With him the inhabitants of a kingdom are divided into the ruling and the ruled. The former class comprises the king and the several ministers whom he of his sovereign pleasure appoints to various posts; and the latter comprises all the rest of the population. Now the relation in which the common people stand to the ruler resembles that of children to a father. They have no part or lot in the administration of government. They are regarded, not as individuals, but as masses. They are the "hundred surnames," or "the people," and the ruler of supreme virtue and wisdom—the godlike man—regards them all impartially as so many straw-made dog-effigies, creatures made to be used. The subjects imitate their king or chief; and as he is, so are they; and excellence in him is followed by excellence in them. The relations of the members of the community to each other are referred, as has been stated, to the province of ethics.

From the above sketch of the political sentiments contained in the *Tao-tĕ Ching*, I hope it has been seen that the author was not an utterly vain dreamer and theoriser, at least on these matters. It would be very easy to show how many of the Confucianist doctrines in politics closely resemble those of Lao-tzŭ; though others, also, are diametrically opposite. The teachings of the latter sage, in point of practicability at least, are not far removed from those of the former.

In many points Lao-tzŭ seems to us to be giving bad advice to the ruler, and his general notions about a state are very unlike those to which we are accustomed. That the people should be kept ignorant, advancement in mechanical skill discountenanced, and that the standards of political excellence should be the ideal sages of an ideal antiquity, are doctrines to which we would refuse to adhere, and which we would condemn, as savouring of despotism. Yet Lao-tzŭ's conception of the ruler is not of him as a despot, but rather as a sort of dictator during good conduct. He is raised to his high position by the concurrent wishes of heaven and the people, and on his observance of the duties of his office depends his stability on the throne. It is interesting and instructive to compare Lao-tzŭ's ideas on politics with those of Macchiavelli, who somewhat resembles him also in his fortunes. Each lived in times of national disaster and misery and each wished for peace in the land. Each longed to see one ruler installed, and honoured with absolute power. During life neither seems to have been appreciated by his fellows; and after death so ill were the merits of both recognised, that the abbreviated form of the Christian name of the one became, as some suppose, a familiar term for the original Devil;[6] and the other has been confounded by his enemies with charlatans and impostors. The counsels which each gave to the chiefs of the time were those which he deemed useful and practicable, though in many cases, if judged by a general standard, they must be condemned. The patriotic fire of the Florentine Secretary led him to make rather reckless statements about the license allowed to the man who makes and keeps himself an absolute and independent prince.[7] So the Chinese moralist, deprecating the evils wrought in his country by unprincipled but clever and ambitious men, recommends a general state of ignorance. The serpent wisdom of the professional statesman, however, is far removed from the guileless simplicity of the philosopher.

6 See Macaulay's Essays, Vol. I., Essay 2.
7 See The Prince, chs. 8, 178.

The latter abbors the idea of war, and recoils from the
thought of force and ostentation ; but the former, with more
earthly prudence, recommends above all things a good native
army, serviceable military skill, and splendid enterprises.[8]
Macchiavelli allows the prince to break his word when
it suits him for state purposes[9] (unless this be ironical), but
Lao-tzŭ requires of the king good faith, at least to his subjects. Each of them advises that the ruler should be, or at
least appear to be, clement and liberal, sparing of the people's
possessions and a fosterer of their material prosperity.[1] Many
other points of similarity or contrast in the political opinions
of these two eminent men might be adduced, but the above
must suffice as examples.

When we read Lao-tzŭ's sentiments about taxation, over-
legislation, penal retributions and excessive governmental
interference, and remember that these same subjects are still
eagerly debated among Western philosophers and statesmen,
we must ascribe to the Chinese sage a remarkable amount of
what Humboldt calls the presentiment of knowledge. What
he, however, could sketch only in faint outline on these
subjects, has been broadly discussed in later and more auspicious times by men like Adam Smith, Bentham, Emerson
and J. S. Mill. If we *now* cannot but condemn his ignoring
the individuality of each member of the state, his discourag-
ing progress in the mechanical arts, and his magnifying
the kingly office, we must remember that there are still
among us, notwithstanding the experience and struggles of
centuries, almost as great barriers to the enjoyment of

8 See *The Prince*, ch. 14.

9   Do.   ch. 18.

1 Ch. 16, &c.

personal liberty as were those which Lao-tzŭ recommends. Large standing armies at the call of one man—"incognoscibility" of the laws—bribery—gerrymandering—and, above all, the power of the many—are still great retarders of human freedom and prosperity. That such things exist, even though the voice of the philosopher is always against them, should make us indulgent towards the mistaken notions of a man who lived 2,500 years ago.

· CHAPTER VII.

ETHICS.

Lao-tzŭ's notions on ethics are fortunately set forth with much more fulness than on any other department of knowledge, and in giving a brief account of them one is rather encumbered by the abundance of aphorisms than perplexed by their paucity. In saying this, however, I do not mean to intimate that the philosopher has elaborated a system of speculative or practical morality, or that he has given full and explicit statements about the moral sense and many other subjects familiar to the student of western ethics. On several of these points he is absolutely silent, and his notions about others are expressed darkly and laconically, and only occasionally in a connected manner. We must, however, make the most we can of the obscure text and discordant commentaries, in order to learn at least an outline of what our author taught.

In the first place, Lao-tzŭ seems to have believed in the existence of a primitive time, when virtue and vice were unknown terms.[1] During this period everything that man

---

1 See chs. 2, 38, and compare the words of Pascal—"la vraie morale se moque de la morale, c'est à dire que la morale du jugement se moque de la morale de l'esprit qui est sans règle." Pensées, Art. xxv., 56.

did was according to Nature (Tao), and this not by any
effort on man's part, but merely as the result of his existence.
He knew not good or evil, nor any of the relative virtues
and vices which have since obtained names. This was the
period of Nature in the world's history, a period of extreme
simplicity of manners and purity of life corresponding to the
Garden-of-Eden state of the Hebrews, before man perceived
that he was unclothed, and became as a God knowing good
and evil. To this succeeded the period of Virtue (德) in
two stages or degrees. The higher is almost identical with
the state of Nature, as in it also man led a pure life, without
need of effort and without consciousness of goodness. Of the
people of this period we may speak as the

"Saturni gentem, haud vinclo nec legibus æquam,
Sponte sua, veterisque dei se more tenentem."[3]

In the next and lower stage life was still virtuous, though
occasionally sliding into vice, and unable to maintain the
stability of unconscious and unforced excellence.[1]   Then
came the time when humanity and equity appeared, and
when filial piety and integrity made themselves known.[4]
These were degenerate days when man was no more "Nature's
priest" and when the "vision splendid" had almost ceased to
attend him.   Finally came the days when craft and cunning
were developed, and when insincerity arose.   Propriety

2 Æneid, B. 7, vv. 203-4.

3 Compare Carlyle,—"Already to the popular judgment, he who
talks much about virtue in the abstract, begins to be suspect," &c. Essay
on Characteristics. So also Emerson writes—"Our moral nature is
vitiated by any interference of our will." Essays, Vol. I., p. 119.

4 See chs. 18, 38.

and carefulness of external deportment also, according to Lao-tzŭ, indicated a great falling away from primitive simplicity the beginning of trouble; and he, accordingly, speaks of them rather slightingly. This is a point on which Confucius seems to have been of a very different opinion, although he had studied the ceremonial code under Lao-tzŭ.

Such is, according to the Tao-tĕ Ching, the mode in which the world gradually became what it is at present. The book does not contain any express statement of opinion as to whether each human creature is born with a good or a bad nature. From various passages in it, however, we are authorised in inferring that Lao-tzŭ regarded an infant as good by nature. Its spirit comes pure and perfect from the Great Mother, but susceptible to all the evil influences which operate upon it and lead it astray.

The standard of virtue to which Lao-tzŭ refers is Nature (Tao), just as another old philosopher says, "in hoc sumus sapientes, quod naturam optimam ducem, tanquam deum, sequimur eique paremus."[5] By our philosopher, however, Nature is not regarded as personified and deified, but is contemplated as the eternal, spontaneous, and emanatory cause. The manifestation of complete virtue comes from Nature only.[6] This is the guide and model of the universe, and it

5 The words of Cato in Cic. De Senectute.

6 Compare Emerson: "The Supreme Critic on the errors of the past and the present, and the only prophet of that which must be, is that great Nature in which we rest, as the earth lies in the soft arms of the atmosphere; that Unity, that Oversoul, within which every man's particular being is contained and made one with all others; that common heart, of which all sincere conversation is the worship, to which all right action is submission; that overpowering reality which confutes our tricks

itself has spontaneity as guide, that is, it has no guide
whatever. All creatures and man among them, must conform
to it or they miss the end of their existence and soon cease
to be. As Tao, however, is very indefinite and intangible,
Lao-tzŭ holds it out to mortals as their guide chiefly through
the medium of certain other ideas more easily comprehended.
Thus Heaven, corresponding somewhat to our notions of
providence, imitates Nature, and becomes to man its visible
embodiment.[7] In its perfect impartiality, its noiseless work-
ing, its disinterested and unceasing well-doing, it presents a
rule by which man should regulate his life.[8] Not less are
the material heavens above him a model in their unerring,
and spontaneous obedience to Nature, and in their eternal
purity. The Earth[9] also, with her calm eternal repose, and
the great rivers and seas, are types of the far-off olden times,
whose boundless merit raised them to the height of fellow-
workers with Nature, and to whom all things once paid a
willing homage, are patterns for all after ages.[1]

Of a personal deity above all these our author makes no
mention, nor can it be inferred with certainty from his book
whether he believed in the existence of such a being. In
one place he speaks of Nature (Tao) as being antecedent

and talents, and constrains every one to pass for what he is, and to
speak from his character, and not from his tongue, and which evermore
tends to pass into our thought and hand, and become wisdom, and
virtue, and power and beauty." Essays, Vol. I., p. 244.

7 Chs. 30, 55.

8 Chs. 7, 77.

9 Ch. 25.

1 Chs. 15, 69. Compare the saying of Sir T. Browne—"Live by
old ethicks and the classical rules of honesty."

to the manifestation of Tĭ (帝), a word which the commentators usually explain as meaning lord or master of
heaven.[2] The learned Dr. Medhurst translates the passage
in question thus, "I do not know whose son it (viz., Taóu)
is ; it is prior to the (Supreme) Ruler of the visible (heavens).
I do not understand how, after this, the same author can state
that the Taoists, that is, with Lao-tzŭ at their head, understand the word Tĭ "in the sense of the Supreme Being."[3]
Ghosts and Spirits (鬼 and 神) are referred to in the Tao-
tĕ Ching, but these are very subordinate beings capable of
being controlled by the saints of the earth. Lao-tzŭ refers,
however, as has been seen, to a supernatural punisher of
crime ; and in several passages he speaks of heaven in a
manner very similar to that in which we do when we mean
thereby the Deity who presides over heaven and earth.[4] Yet
we must not forget that it is inferior and subsequent to the
mysterious Tao, and in fact produced by the latter. I cannot,
accordingly, agree with the learned Pauthier when he writes
thus about the Sixteenth Chapter of the Tao-tĕ Ching—"Ce
chapitre renferme à lui seul les éléments d'une religion ; et
il n'est pas étonnant que les Sectateurs de Lao-tseu, si habiles,
comme tous les Asiatiques, à tirer d'un principe posé toutes
les conséquences qui en découlent logiquement, aient établi
un culte et un sacerdoce avec les doctrines du philosophe ;
car dès l'instant qu'un Dieu suprême est annoncé, que les
bonnes actions et la connaissance que l'on acquiert de lui sont
les seuls moyens pour l'homme de parvenir a l'éternelle

2 Ch. 4. The word *Asiang* 象 is also explained here as meaning
probably or *it seems*; the equivalent of *ya* (猶).

3 Dissertation on the Theology of the Chinese, &c., p. 246.

4 Chs. 73, 77.

félicité dans son sein, il est bien évident qu'il faut des médiateurs entre ce Dieu et l'homme pour conduire et éclairer les intelligences ignorantes et faibles."[5] Tao with Lao-tzŭ is not a deity, but is above all deities, and, as has been seen, it is not always represented unchangeable. On the contrary, regarded from one point of view the Tao is in a state of constant change—"twinkling restlessly," to use an expression from Wordsworth. Only when considered as the existence which was solitary in the universe and eternal, is it spoken of as unchanging. Long after Lao-tzŭ's time Tao was, indeed, raised or rather degraded to be a deity, but the theories of later Taoists are seldom the logical developments of the doctrines of Lao-tzŭ, and in this they err widely.

Of virtue in the abstract little is said by our author, but we know that his idea of it was that it consisted in following Nature (Tao). He generally, however, speaks of it in the concrete as the perfect nature of the world or man and the other creatures of the universe. Sometimes indeed he refers to Tĕ, Virtue, as if it were a mysterious, independent existence and not an inherent quality. At other times he seems to regard good and bad as merely relative terms, the existence of the former implying and indeed causing the existence of the latter, and vice versâ.

Descending from these generalities, however, we now come to the consideration of Lao-tzŭ's conception of the ideal sage. The virtues which characterise the perfect man, and which all should endeavour to possess, are described in the Tao-tĕ Chīng with greater or less fulness. Among the most important of these is the negative excellence of an

5 China, pp. 116-7.

absence of the bustling ostentation of goodness. Not to be
fussy or showy, but to do one's proper work and lead a
quiet life without meddling in the concerns of others, are
virtues which to Lao-tzŭ seemed of transcendent importance.
the expression which I interpreted as meaning absence of
ostentation or bustle is *wu wei* (無 爲).[6] Many Chinese
commentators seem to regard this as equivalent to nothingness, non-existence, or absolute inaction; so Julien also
translates it usually by " non-agir."[7] Though, however, the
words have in many places these meanings, yet there are
several passages which seem to require the explanation
given above, and which is also in harmony with the general
tenor of the book. Man's guide is Nature (Tao), and it
works incessantly but without noise or show. So also it is
not an inactive life that Lao-tzŭ commends, but a gentle
one, and one which does not obtrude itself on the notice of
the world. The man who would follow Nature must try to
live virtuously without the appearance of so doing; he must
present a mean exterior while under it he hides the inestim-
able jewel.[8] The advice which Sir Thomas Browne gives
is very like the teaching of Lao-tzŭ. "Be substantially great
in thyself, and more than thou appearest unto others; and
let the world be deceived in thee, as they are in the lights
of heaven."[9] Again, the man who follows Nature is wise

6 See chs. 2, &c. Wei (爲) sometimes means to esteem, and Wei-
wu-wei would then mean to esteem without appearing to do so. Compare
Shi-wu-shi (事無事), Shang-tĕ pu-tĕ (上德不德), &c.

7 In this he is often followed by Mr. Chalmers. Pauthier also so
translates the expression.

8 See chs. 41, 70.

9 Christian Morals, Section xix.

but wears the mask of ignorance [1]—to the world he appears
silly and stupid, but in his breast are deep stores of wisdom.
So also he does good without the show of doing it; he helps
in the amelioration of his fellows, and indeed of all things
in the world, without talking or making any display.[2] He
does his alms not before men but in secret and without a
preluding trumpet. Those are rare who can instruct others
without the necessity of talking, and benefit them without
making a show; but in striving to attain to this excellence
man is aiming at the perfection of Nature.[3] The art of
living thus is an art made by Nature "—the, silent, informing,
universally-operant spirit. By Nature (Tao) the passions
and other impediments to virtue are lessened more and more

1 So Celsus represents the early Christians as saying—" Wisdom is a
bad thing in life, foolishness is to be preferred." Neander, Ch. Hist.,
Vol. I., p. 164 (Amer. Translation).

2 See chs. 45, 71, 77. Compare the statement attributed to Gotama
Buddha. " Great King, I do not teach the law to my pupils, telling
them, Go, ye saints, and before the eyes of the Brahmans and house-
holders perform, by means of your supernatural powers, miracles
greater than any man can perform. I tell them, when I teach
them the law, Live, ye saints, hiding your good works, and showing
your sins." Chips from a German Workshop, Vol. I., p. 249;
translated from Burnouf, Introduction à l'Histoire du Buddhisme
Indien, p. 170.

3 Compare Emerson—" The man may teach by doing, and not
otherwise. If he can communicate himself he can teach, but not by
word." Essay IV., Vol. I., p. 136.

4 Ch. 43.

until man attains to that state of perfection in which he acts naturally and so can do all things.[5]

The virtue of humility is one of which Lao-tzŭ speaks very highly. Water is always with him the type of what is humble; and the godlike man, like it, occupies a low position, which others abhor but in which he can profit all around him.[6] "The supremely virtuous is like water," are words taken from the Tao-tĕ Ching, and frequently inscribed on rocks and other objects. Such a man does not claim precedence or merit, nor does he strive with any one.[7] He never arrogates honour or preferment, yet they come to him;[8] and he is yielding and modest, yet always prevails in the end. When success is obtained, and his desire accomplished, he modestly retires. Pride, on the other hand, and vaulting ambition, always fail to attain the wished-for consummation.[9] So also the man who is violent and headstrong generally comes to a bad end.[1] Some of the commentators, however, seem to take this humility in a bad sense, and they would make us believe that the quality as recommended by Lao-tzŭ is not virtue but rather a vice, as partaking of the nature of a trick or artifice. The historical instance which they most frequently quote as illustrating the

5 Ch. 48. *Wu-wei* here may have another meaning. Wu-ch'ĕng and Jullen regard it as meaning *inaction*, and make it synonymous with *Wu-shi*. See Mr. Chalmers' extraordinary translation of this chapter.

6 Chs. 8, 78.

7 Chs. 22, 34, 66.

8 Compare the saying of Solomon,—"Before honour is humility." Proverbs, xviii. 12.

9 See chs. 92, 24.

1 Ch. 42.

success of this humility is the career of the famous Chang Tzŭ-fang ,張子房), a sort of political Uriah Heep.

To continence also Lao-tzŭ assigns a high place. The total exemption from the power of the passions and desire is a moral pre-eminence to which man should seek to attain—

"For not to desire or admire, if a man could learn it, were more

Than to walk all day like the Sultan of old in a garden of spice."

It is the body, with its inseparably connected emotions and passions, which is the cause of all the ills that attend humanity;[2] and he who would return to the state of original innocence must overcome his body.[3]   To be without desires is to be at rest, and if man were freed from the body he would have no cause for fear.   To keep the gateways of the senses closed against the sight, sounds and tastes which distract and mar the soul within, is the simple metaphor which Lao-tzŭ uses to express this overcoming of self.[4]   This conquest he puts above every other.   He who knows others is learned, but he who knows himself is enlightened; he who overcomes others has physical force, but he who overcomes himself has moral strength.[5]   The disastrous consequence of yielding to the bodily appetites is beautifully illustrated by a metaphor familiar to us in a Taoist book to

2 Ch. 18.

3 Ch. 37.

4 Chs. 52, 56.

5 Ch. 83. Compare the words of Sir T. Browne : —" Rest not in an ovation, but a triumph over thy passions." Christian Morals, sect. 2. So also Solomon—" He that is slow to anger is better than the mighty ; and he that ruleth his spirit than he that taketh a city." Proverbs, xvi. 82.   Compare also Horace's Ode to Sallust, vs. 9, &c.

which I have already referred. The people of the world
following their desires strive for reputation, grasp at gain,
covet wine, and lust after beauty—they take the bitter for
the pleasant and the false for the real—day and night they
toil and moil, morn and even they fret and care, nor desist
even when their vital energies are almost exhausted. Like
the moth which extinguishes its life in the dazzling blaze of
the lamp or the worm which goes to its own destruction in
the fire, these men do not wait for the command of the king
of Death, but send themselves to the grave.[6]

Associated with continence is the virtue of moderation,
which also must form part of the good man's character. To
be content is to be rich and brings with it no danger or
shame, while there is no greater calamity than not to know
when to be satisfied.[7] He who knows where to stop will not
incur peril, nor will he ever indulge in excess. To fill a cup
while holding it in the hand is not so good as to let it alone,
or, as we say, it is hard to carry a full cup even.[8] Too
sharp an edge cannot be kept on a tool, and a hall full of
gold and precious stones cannot be defended; and he who
is wanton in prosperity leaves a legacy of misfortune. Various
other metaphors are used to inculcate the necessity of following the mean, and abstaining from extravagance. The man
who erects himself on tiptoe cannot continue so, nor can he
who takes long strides continue to walk.[9] The intelligent

6 悟道錄. Ch. 2, p. 11.

7 See Chs. 33, 44, 40, 29, 32.

8 Ch. 9. Compare Horace's advice :—" Quod satis est cui contigit,
hic nihil amplius optet."

9 Ch. 24.

and good man will be moderate in all things, not desiring to
be prized like jade or slighted like a stone.[1]

It is also a characteristic of the truly virtuous man that
he is always, and especially in privacy, grave and serious,
and not unmindful of his weak points. He who knows his
strength and protects his weakness at the same time will
have all the world resorting to him for instruction and
example; eternal virtue will not leave him, and he will
return to the natural goodness of infancy.[2] Many things
fail when the goal is nearly attained, but the godlike man is
careful about the end no less than about the beginning.[3] So
also were the sages of antiquity whose cautious, hesitating
character is portrayed in outline as a model for others.[4]

Mercy is another virtue to which Lao-tzŭ attaches considerable importance. Nor is the quality of mercy, as he
represents it, strained within any narrow compass. On the
contrary, it flows not only over all mankind, but even to the
entire world. As has been seen, Lao-tzŭ would have all
capital punishment reserved for a supernatural agent to
execute, and he would have the correction of wickedness
effected by the quiet influence of a good example. He goes
farther than this, however; for he will have us to abstain
from even judging others—from dividing men into the
righteous and the sinners.[5] It is Heaven alone which is
to determine the moral worth of human creatures, and give
to each his meed. And we must not even assign worldly
misfortunes to the displeasure of Heaven—must not say that
the eighteen on whom the tower of Siloam fell were greater

1 Ch. 39.   5 Chs. 19, 78.
2 Chs. 26, 28.   4 Ch. 15.
3 Chs. 63, 64.

sinners than the other residents in Jerusalem. The good
man must not only not think too harshly of the man who is
not good,[6] but he must even love him, and must reward
ill will by virtue—the *ne plus ultra* of generosity, as one of
the commentators observes.[7] So also the feeling of compassion will cause the good man to keep his good qualities in the
back ground, and not excite the evil passions of the bad
man by displaying them obtrusively before him. After a
great dispute has been adjusted some grudge is sure to
remain, so to live peaceably is to be regarded as virtuous.[8]
The good man keeps his proof of an agreement, but he does
not claim from the other party to it the fulfillment of the
agreement, that is, he will not sue him at a court of law.
This spirit of mercy and compassion ought not only to
prevail in private and social life, but it ought to extend also
to the seat of power and even to temper the fierce passions
of warfare. Then from the circle of humanity Lao-tsŭ looks
abroad over the ample spaces of nature, and extends to them
also a kindly sympathy. The good man never injures anything in the world; on the contrary he saves the inferior
creatures and assists them in their ever-renewed operations
of coming into existence, growing, and returning to their

6 Ch. 27. The word *shan* (善), however, rendered *good*, is also
susceptible of the interpretation *clever* or *expert*. See Wu-ch'ing's note
(ch. 22 in his edition).

7 Ch. 63. In the Kan-ying-p'ien (感應篇) it is said "Look
on the acquisitions of others as if they were yours, and the losses of others
as if they were yours." Ch. 2. In this book are taught many other
excellent lessons which are apparently derived from the Tao-tŏ Ching.

8 Ch. 79.

original source.[9] Did the whole creation in his eyes, too, groan and travail in pain?

Of courage, truth, honesty, and several other virtues Lao-tzŭ does not make much mention. He seems also to think lightly of conventional humanity and equity, but Han Wên Kung says this was because he had a low conception of these two virtues. According to the figure used by Han, Lao-tzŭ was as a man sitting at the bottom of a well and pronouncing the sky to be of small dimensions.[1] He teaches, however, the mutual dependence of man upon man, and the consequent necessity of the interchange of good offices. The good man gives and asks not—does good and looks not for recompense. He who is virtuous is master of him who is not virtuous, but respect and affection must exist between them. The ruler and the ruled also are mutually dependent, and they too must reciprocate kindness and forbearance.

Lao-tzŭ repeatedly condemns the vices of much and fine talking. The wise man, he says, does not talk, and to do without audible words is to follow Nature.[2] Man ought to be silent in his actions as is the all-working Nature. Faithful words are not fine, and fine words are not faithful: the virtuous man is not argumentative and *vice versâ*.

To learning and wisdom our author does not, I think, assign a sufficiently high place, but seems rather to condemn

9 See chs. 27, 64. So the Kan-ying-p'ien says:—"The tiny insects and plants and trees may not be injured."

1 Works, ch. 11, 原道.

2 Chs. 23, 56. Compare "Let us be silent, for so are the gods." Also the words of the Tatler:—"Silence is sometimes more significant and sublime than the most noble and most expressive eloquence, and is on many occasions the indication of a great mind." No. 133.

them.[3] Learning adds to the evils of existence, and if we could put it away we would be exempt from anxiety. The ancient rulers kept the people ignorant and they had good government—so the people ought still to be kept in ignorance. But perhaps Lao-tzŭ refers to the faults of those persons who drink only slightly of the Pierian spring and then boast of what they acquire, thereby doing injury to themselves and to society. It would, however, have been better if he had distinguished between the pretenders to knowledge, and those who have drunk deeply at the fountain of wisdom by assigning to intellectual worth its proper importance.[4]

Lao-tzŭ, as has been seen, is not unmindful of the infirmity of noble minds which expects a recompense for a virtuous life. Nor are the inducements which he holds out of a slight or unworthy nature. On the contrary, they are to souls which have begun to delight in the path of virtue, and also to those still walking in "error's wandering wood," calculated to have a great effect. The desires and appetites must all be overcome and self must be subdued, but to him who obtains the victory there remain grand prizes. The gateways of knowledge are open to him, and he can contemplate the mysterious operations of nature.[5] Fame and greatness come to him unsolicited, and the years of his life are increased. Having the guileless purity of an infant—becoming like a little child—he will enjoy an exemption from the fear of noxious

3 Chs. 65, 20, 48.

4 Compare Emerson. Essays vol. i., p. 281-2.

6 Ch. 1. Chalmers, however, translates—"In eternal non-existence, therefore, man seeks to pierce the primordial mystery, and in eternal existence, to behold the issues of the Universe." See also the German translation given in Hegel, Geschichte, &c. Vol. I., p. 142.

animals and wicked men.[6] Fierce beasts cannot gore or tear
him, nor the soldier wound him in battle, that is, having
perfect love towards all things he will not fear harm from
any.[7] The godlike man does not use his neighbour as a foil
to set off his own excellence, but rather assimilates himself
to all. Thus he comes into intimate union with his fellow-
creatures and is set on high without incurring any ill-will.
He lives not for himself but for others, and his life is pro-
longed by so doing. He does not amass for himself, nor
does he bury his talent in the barren ground of itself. He
spends it in the service of his fellows and it comes back to
him with interest.[8] The more he serves the more he has
wherewith to serve, and the more he gives the richer he
becomes. It is almost surprising to find this thought thus
expressed by Lao-tzŭ, and the words of one of his disciples,
following out the idea, are somewhat remarkable—" There
is also accumulation which causes deficiency, and a non-
hoarding which results in having something over."[9] There
are several passages in the Tao-tê Ching besides the above,
which might be included among the " testimonia animæ
naturaliter Christianæ." Humility, charity, and the forgive-
ness of injuries which are sometimes spoken of as purely
Christian virtues are certainly inculcated by Lao-tzŭ.[1] But
to return to our subject.—Man's life ought thus to be continued opposition to self, gaining more and more control
over it, until the passions cease to trouble and self is per-

6 Chs. 7, 59.

7 Chs. 50, 55.

8 See chs. 66, 7, 81.

9 Quoted by Wu-ch'êng in a note to ch. 81.

1 Compare Pauthier. Chine, p. 117.

fectly vanquished. Then comes the end which crowns the
work. When the fleshly appetites have been subdued, and
the spirit has attained that state in which it is

—" equable and pure ;
No fears to beat away—no strife to heal—
The past unsighed for, and the future sure,"

then comes death. And what after death ? Man returns to
Nature, which delights to receive him, and identifies him
with her own mysterious self. Hither, too, come all the
myriad things which had once emanated from the womb
of the same all-producing mother. This in reality means that
man and all other creatures return to nothingness. This
is the dreamless sleep wherewith our life is rounded—this is
the end of all our woe and misery, to be

—" Swallowed up and lost
In the wide womb of uncreated night
Devoid of sense and motion."

There is at least one passage in which Lao-tzŭ seems to
speak of a life after death,[2] but this passage presents great
difficulties, and perhaps refers only to the " fancied life
in others' breath" by which a man though dead is not lost.
That man loses his individuality and that he loses his existence
are two doctrines strongly opposed to Lao-tzŭ. The individual
is everything with the one, nothing with the other.[3] As to
the immortality of the soul, this is a doctrine of which many
other excellent philosophers before the rise of Christianity
had little or no conception. We are wont to regard the
theory of the soul's mortality as dismal and hopeless; yet

2 Ch. 23. See Pauthier. Chine Moderne, ps. 356-7.

3 Emerson, however, also speaks of the "individual soul mingling
with the Universal Soul." Essays.

Lao-tzŭ holds out the hope of annihilation or at least of
absorption into universal Nature as the highest reward for a
life of untiring virtue. Few, he says, understand the matter ;
and few as yet even understand the meaning of the immortality of the soul. The belief that the soul is mortal no less
than the opposite belief seems to lead to the possession of a
calm, contented spirit, and an indifference to the things of
this life. The strange but eloquent words of the Hydriota-
phia on this subject will form the closing sentence of this
chapter :—" And if any have been so happy as truly to
understand Christian annihilation, ecstasies, exolution, lique-
faction, transformation, the kiss of the spouse, gustation of
God, and ingression into the divine shadow; they have already
had an handsome anticipation of heaven ; the glory of the
world is surely over, and the earth in ashes unto them." [4]

4 Ch. 5.

CHAPTER VIII.

LAO-TZŬ AND CONFUCIUS.

It is not unusual for foreigners no less than for Chinese to speak of Lao-tzŭ and Confucius as having lived on very bad terms with each other and as having been diametrically opposite in their teachings. One Chinese scholar who ought to have known much better sins very badly in this respect. The excellent little book of Mr Edkins on the Religious Condition of the Chinese contains the following: "Contemporary with Confucius, there was an old man afterwards known as Laou-tsoo, who meditated in a philosophic mood upon the more profound necessities and capacities of the human soul. He did so in a way that Confucius, the prophet of the practical, could not well comprehend. He conversed with him once, but never repeated his visit, for he could not understand him. Laou-tsoo recommended quiet reflection. Water that is still is also clear, and you may see deeply into it. Noise and passion are fatal to spiritual progress. The stars are invisible through a clouded sky. Nourish the perceptive powers of the soul in purity and rest."[1] Others. have expressed a similar opinion and with no more accuracy.

1 Page 9.

This view, however, is not strictly correct. As has been
seen, Confucius was a disciple of Lao-tzŭ, and there is no
evidence to prove that any other than friendly relations
existed between them. A Confucianist philosopher has
somewhere remarked that Confucius and Lao-tzŭ were not
the authors of opposite systems and founders of rival schools
of philosophy, and the observation is quite correct. It was
not until long after the two sages were dead that the followers
of the one came to look on those of the other as heretics
and enemies. Not only, however, did Confucius himself
live in friendship with his instructor, so far as we know, but
he also imbibed not a few of his tenets. The influence of
Lao-tzŭ on his disciple, and the amount of similarity between
the doctrines of the two are subjects well deserving a serious
study. That they differ widely on many points is a fact
known to everybody, but few, so far as my knowledge
extends, have studied the affinities between them. To a
thorough-going Confucianist the mere idea of doing such a
a thing is horrible, and the Temple of Literature closed
against the reception of the tablets of the rare individuals
who have essayed the task, deters the after generations. By
one, however, not anxious about his posthumous tablet, and
who takes pleasure in finding how near the divergent lines
of orthodoxy and heterodoxy may be found to have originally
converged, the work may be attempted without any mis-
givings. The present writer can do nothing more than merely
try to sketch a few of the features of resemblance between
the teachings of the two sages in speculative Physics, Politics
and Ethics, following the division adopted above.

The theories of Lao-tzŭ and Confucius on the physical
world being probably merely the popular and traditional
notions of the time, might naturally be expected to have not

a little in common. For example, the emanation of the
visible universe, including also all that makes up man, from
an eternal existence at once material and immaterial, seems
to have been an old idea with the Chinese, and it is found
in the teachings of both the sages. Thus, as has been seen,
the Tai-chi (太極) or Grand Extreme, as it is translated,
is only Tao under another name. Indeed Confucius uses
the latter word in this connection very much after the
manner of Lao-tzŭ. In the appendix to the Yi-ching (易繫)
it is stated that what is antecedent to external form is called
Tao;[2] and in another passage it is said that one passive and
one active element (one Yin and one Yang) are called Tao.[3]
In the Li-Chi (禮記) Confucius says to Tzŭ-kung that Tao
is that which the whole world, (天下 may also mean the
empire), esteems.[4] Other writers also, such as the author of
the preface to the Yi-ching, distinctly assert that the two
terms Tai-chi and Tao have the same signification. Lao-tzŭ's
doctrine of dualism also, and his theory that contraries
produce each other are found explicitly taught in the Confucian classics. Thus the Yi-ching says that hard and soft
alternately thrust each other forth,[5] and in another passage
it is said that the Yin and the Yang, or the passive and
active elements or powers of nature, generate each other.
Again Lao-tzŭ teaches that all the operations of Nature
(Tao) and Heaven and earth are carried on without any
show of effort, silently and quietly. So also does Confucius
teach. In the Li-chi, for example, he says that the Tien-

2 Vol. II , Appendix, ch. 12.

3 Vol. B , Appendix, ch. 5.

4 Ch. 10, page 65, compare also the Chung-Yung, ch. 27.

5 Vol. E., Appendix, ch. 2.

tao or Way of Heaven is to be without exertion and yet
have the world completed.[6] In the Chung-yung a similar
observation is made respecting Ch'êng (誠) which Legge
translates "sincerity" but which is evidently another designation of Tao, as Mr Meadows long ago stated.[7] Further, it is
almost unnecessary to state that in the quinary classification
of such things as tastes and colours our two sages perfectly
agree. Not only, however, do we find the same ideas on
these matters in Confucian classics and the Tao-tê Ching but
we also not seldom find in them similar forms of expression.[8]
Thus, for instance, the poetical metaphor by which Lao-tzŭ
speaks of the sea and the great rivers as being kings to the
small streams which flow into them is found in the Shu-
King and the Shi Khing. In the former the Chiang (江)
and Han (漢) are described as proceeding to the sovereign
Court of the Sea,[9] and in the latter it is written that the full
tide flows back to pay court to the sea, but the people of
the country forget their allegiance. It may be mentioned
that we ourselves speak of *tributary* streams, and Tennyson
has expressed the Chinese idea fully in the words

" Flow down, cold rivulet, to the sea,
Thy tribute wave deliver."

Coming now to Politics we find that on Government and
other matters connected with the State, the Confucian writings

6 Ch. 9, p. 6. See also the remarks of Callery in his note to this
passage. Li-ki, p. 142.

7 Chinese Classics, vol. i , p. 282 3-4. The Chinese and their Rebellions, p. 851.

8 Compare Yi-ching, Vol. ii., Appendix, ch. 11, with the Tao-tê
ching, ch. 6.

9 Legge's Shu, vol. L, p. 113.

contain many opinions closely resembling those of Lao-tzŭ.
Thus in the Lun Yŭ, Book xv., Confucius is represented as
saying—"May not Shun be instanced as having governed
efficiently without exertion? What did he do? He did
nothing but gravely and reverently occupy his imperial
seat." Here the very expression of the Tao-tê Ching is
used—無爲而治—and Dr. Legge has, I think, rightly
translated wu-wei by "without exertion."[1] So also in the
Shu King it is said of King Wu, after his war with Shou
was finished, that "he had only to let his robes fall down,
and fold his hands, and the empire was orderly ruled."[2]
Other passages in the Lun-yŭ show us that Confucius also
disliked war, and the petty squabbles into which the ambitious feudal chiefs of his time were constantly falling.
Again, Lao-tzŭ has been greatly reproached by Confucianists
and others for declining to continue in office under the
kings of Chow, but he went little farther in this respect than
his more fortunate disciple who was more earthly wise
though less politically consistent. Each kept his precious
gem secreted for years, but there was this difference, that
Confucius was eager for a bidder who would please him,
and Lao-tzŭ seeing there was no chance of a suitable bidder
preferred to keep his gem. Not only, however, did Confucius himself abstain for a considerable time from active
official life, but he also commended those of the past and
some of his contemporaries who had retired into privacy
during evil times, and his approbation of Ning-wu's conduct
is expressed in language worthy of Lao-tzŭ.[3] Besides, Con-

---

1 Chinese Classics, vol. 1, p. 159.

2 Legge's Shu King, vol. li., p. 316.

3 Legge's Ch. Classics, vol. i., p. 44.

fucius had the utmost contempt for the mandarins and chiefs of his time, and regarded them as either utter villains or as mere nobodies.[4] Again, just as Lao-tzŭ teaches that the ruler must first correct himself, making the purity of his own inner life his first and greatest care and then cultivating moral excellence in his family, so Confucius repeatedly teaches the same doctrine and illustrates it by the example of the ancients. Like ruler like people, is a maxim with him. If the sovereign be wicked the people also will be wicked, and if he be good they also will be good.[5] Lao-tzŭ says that government must be conducted by uprightness or rectitude (正). So Confucius says that to govern means to rectify, and in another passage he depicts the evil results of a government which is not conducted in uprightness. Another political doctrine which is stated expressly in the Tao-tĕ Ching is that capital punishment is the work of a super-human agent and that no one on earth can safely act as proxy for that agent. Through all the Confucian writings also there runs the idea that it is Heaven or the Upper Ruler that is offended with wicked states, rebellious chiefs, or oppressive rulers, and that all national rewards and punishments come from the same source. Confucius, however, and his followers seem to have believed that the virtuous neighbouring state, the pious sovereign, or the successful rebel received a Heavenly edict to annex the wicked territory, slay the mutinous chief, or dethrone the impious prince—a political idea not confined to ancient times or to China. Yet there are several passages in the Classics which seem to represent Confucius, too, as forbidding, or at least disapprov-

4 See for instance Legge, Ch. Classics, vol. I., p. 136.
5 See Legge, vol. I., ps. 122, 130 ; also the Li Chi, ch. I, p. 52.

ing of, capital punishment. Thus in the Lun-yü he is made
to say to Chi-k'ang, who had asked him about slaying the
bad in order to perfect the good—" Why use capital punishment at all ? Do you desire virtue and the people will be
virtuous. The moral character of the ruler is to that of his
subjects as wind is to grass—when the wind blows the grass
bends." [6] And in another passage he is represented as
approving of an old saying that after good government for
a hundred years capital punishment might be dispensed
with.[7] Another maxim of the Tao-tê Ching also inculcated
by Confucius is this—that the sovereign ought to anticipate
and be prepared for reverses of fortune—that he ought to
devise measures for repressing rebellion while as yet there
is no sign of disturbance ; this, says the Shu King, was the
method pursued by the ancient rulers.[8] So also both sages
taught that the ruler should always be grave and serious,
mindful of the solemn charge which he has received from
Heaven.[9] In the Confucian writings, again, no less than in
the Tao-tê Ching, rulers are forbidden to covet and strive for
rare and outlandish objects, such things having a tendency
to stir up strife and lead the heart astray.[1] Further in the
high pre-eminence assigned to the sovereign, Confucius is of
the same mind with Lao-tzŭ. As the latter ranks him with
Heaven and Earth, so also does the former.[2] In the opinion -
of each he reigns by divine right, and is himself indeed at

6 Legge, &c., vol. i., p. 122.
7 Legge, &c., vol. i., p. 131.
8 Legge's Shu King, vol. ii., p. 525.   Vol. i., p. 257.
9 Legge's Shu King, vol. i., p. 74, also vol. ii., p. 532.
1 Legge's Shu King, vol. i., p. 349.   Vol. ii., p. 574.
2 See Li Chi, ch. 8, p. 70.

least half divine. Son of Heaven is a frequent designation
of him in the Classics. Confucius indeed in some places is
much more wildly extravagant in his statements about the
sovereign than we would be inclined to expect. Finally,
to both sages the great and paramount consideration for a
prince or chief seemed to be the peace and prosperity of his
people. Light taxes, few legal restrictions, and a general
kind treatment are strongly recommended by both.[3] They
differ, however, in this respect that while Lao-tzŭ overlooks
or slights education, Confucius regards it as of great importance ; but few who know the nature of the education which
Confucius recommended to his son of carp-derived name,
but which he did not give him, would be disposed to regret
the want of it in a ruler or magistrate.

It now remains to speak of the Ethical teachings of Lao-
tzŭ and Confucius, and here also we find considerable similarity, only a few instances of which can now be indicated.
As Confucius disclaimed the distinction of being original in
his views, I am much inclined to believe that the resemblance
between the doctrines of the classics and those of the Tao-tĕ
Ching often point to a borrowing on the part of the former
from the latter. The low place which is assigned to intellectual and mechanical accomplishment in this work seems
to be wrong, and Confucius would scarcely go so far. He
too, however, places virtue above wisdom, and seems sometimes to think that perfect virtue ensures to its possessor
other and less noble qualities. He is not unmindful of the
value of intellectual acquirements and assigns to them considerable importance. It must be remembered besides that
the accomplishments of which Lao-tzŭ speaks disparagingly

are those more for show than utility, and that in this respect
Confucius is at one with him. The vice of talking specious
and flattering words is condemned by the one as strongly as
by the other. Artful words and a clever appearance are
seldom virtuous, is a sentence which Confucius is represented
as repeating on several occasions.[4] In the Yi-ching it is
said that the good man talks little and the violent man talks
much.[5] Here it is worthy of notice that the word which is
opposed to *chi* (吉), good, is not hsiung (凶), wicked, but
ts'ao (躁), a word which means fierce or violent. Indeed
Confucius insists on the gentle life no less earnestly than
Lao-tzŭ, although he is not always consistent. He also
recommends abstinence from litigation. Like Lao-tzŭ he
teaches that the man of extensive influence ought to abase
himself before others—ought to yield and never wrangle.[6]
On some occasions Confucius is represented as holding the
maxim that what a man would not desire another to do to
him he should not do to others,[7] while he is also represented
as objecting to the words of Lao-tzŭ that injury should be
repaid by kindness.[8] But on the other hand he makes it
one of the characteristics of the Chŭn-tzŭ (君子) or noble
man, that he does not strive, and a yielding, forbearing dis-
position is one of the virtues which admiring disciples have
assigned to "the Master" himself. In connection with this it
may be mentioned that the Confucian writings are as bitter as

4 See Legge, Ch. Classics, vol. L, 166 and p. 3. Compare also the
memorable words in the Li-chi, ch. 9, p. 489.

5 Vol. iL, Appendix, Part 2, ch. 12.

6 See Legge Ch. Classics, vol. i, p. 21.

7 See Legge, vol L, p. 165.

8 See Legge, vol. i., p. 152.

the Tao-tĕ Ching against the show and consciousness of being virtuous. The words of the Emperor Shun to Yü as recorded in the Shu King are very like those of Lao-tzŭ, "Without any prideful presumption, there is no one in the empire to contest with you the palm of ability ; without any boasting, there is no one in the empire to contest with you the claim of merit."[9]

The lofty eminence on which Laó-tzŭ places the God-like man is not greater than that to which Confucius raises him. This person ranks, according to both, with Heaven and Earth, and assists these in their great unceasing labours of producing, nourishing, and ruling the creatures of the universe.[1] With Heaven and Earth he makes a trinity, and is scarcely inferior to them. Like Heaven, which he imitates, he is free from partialities, and is universal in his sympathies.[2] One of the philosophers, Ch'êng, a Confucianist after the most straitest sect, forgets his master's doctrine in this respect and through excess of orthodoxy actually becomes heterodox.[3] Criticising Lao-tzŭ's statement that Heaven, Earth, and the God-like man are pu jen (不 仁), that is, are without any partialities or particular affection, he says that we may make this remark of Heaven and Earth but not of the God-like man who feels for and compassionates his fellow creatures, and thus is able to enlarge his way of life.[4] This author, however, seems to be here guilty of a

9 Legge's Shu King, vol. i., p. 60.   See also Dr. Legge's note on the passage. See also do. p. 257.

1 See Li-chi, ch. 4, p. 52.

2 See Legge's Chinese Classics, vol. i., p. 14.

3 See the 性理標題, ch., 17, p. 2.

4 A quotation from the Lun-yü, B. xv, ch. 28.

sophisma equivocationis, as *jên* in the former part of the paragraph is used in a bad sense while in the latter part it has a good sense. The words of the King of Chow to the newly appointed Chief Hu on this subject are very similar to those of Lao-tzŭ—"Great Heaven has no affections—it helps only the virtuous."[5] So also, as Lao-tzŭ says it is Heaven's way to take from that which has too much and give to that which wants, the *Shu-ching* says in like terms "It is virtue which moves Heaven; there is no distance to which it does not reach. Pride brings loss, and humility receives increase:—this is the way of Heaven."[6]

Again, the doctrine of the Tao-tê Ching, that violence and excess cannot endure, appears also in the Confucian works. It occurs, for instance, in the Li-chi, and it is worthy of observation that the illustrious commentator on the passage regards the expression there used as a quotation, but does not know from what work.[7] Had the words been identical there could not have been any possibility of doubt. There is also a common saying among the Chinese, derived from the Yi-ching, that when the sun has reached his meridian he begins to decline, and when the moon has reached her full she begins to wane, thus intimating the fickleness of fortune. This idea is represented in the Tao-tê Ching under a different figure.

In many passages of the books which go by his name, Confucius is made to impress on his disciples the necessity

5 Legge's Shu king, vol. il., p. 490. See also, vol. L, p. 209.

6 Legge's vol. I., p. 65. Reference is apparently made to the Yi-ching where 謙 and 損 are two of the Diagrams. It is a wonder that this escaped Dr. Legge's notice.

7 See Li-chi, ch. 1, p. 1, and Chu-hsi's note.

of attending to what is unseen and internal, and taking it for
granted that the visible and external will follow as a natural
consequence.[8] In this too he is nearly alike to Lao-tzŭ.
One passage of the Lun-yü even speaks of *Li* (禮), or the
full complement of external virtues, on which Confucius
generally lays great stress as something to be postponed to
the genuine qualities of the heart.[9] The whole of the
thirty-third chapter of the Chung-yung may be regarded
as a sort of commentary on what Lao-tzŭ has said on this
and some other topics. · The passages quoted in this chapter
from the Shi-ching are merely texts which have not the
slightest reference to the homilies on them except in one
or two cases.

Further, as Lao-tzŭ believed in a long-past time of simplicity and purity, so also did Confucius, and his love for
antiquity and his esteem for the ancient sages were perhaps
even greater than those of Lao-tzŭ.[1] Of the five characteristics given of the old kings who had kept good government in their kingdoms the first is that they honoured those
who had Tê (德), that is, their perfect inborn nature, and
this is explained to mean those who approach *Tao*. Both
sages represent the ancients as solid and not showy, as
wanting in intellectual arts but perfect in simple virtue.
They should be, both thought, in the conduct of life no less
than in affairs of State the models for all after generations.
Turn to the good old paths wherein our forefathers walked
who were better than we, is what Lao-tzŭ and Confucius

8 Compare on this, other topics mentioned by Lao-tzŭ, the character
of the 儒 in the Li-chi, ch. 10.

9 Legge's Ch. Classics, vol. I., p. 21.

1 See Legge's Shu, &c., vol. ii., p. 491.

equally teach. Go back, says the latter, to the days of Yao
and Shun, and Yŭ, and kings Wên and Wu, and Duke
Chou, and make them your patterns in all things even as they
made Heaven theirs. Ascend still further, says Lao-tzŭ, and
follow the lives of those primitive worthies who died before
the arts and vices of civilisation had appeared on the
earth.

What the inducements are which Lao-tzŭ holds out to a
life of self-subduing and virtue has been seen already, and
those which the Confucian books hold out to such a life
are very similar.[2] An insight into the mysteries of Providence, length of years, a peaceful death, and a good name
among men are the chief rewards for such a life. Confucius
in one place is represented as making perfect knowledge
precede self-purification.[3] This, however, is not, I think,
in accordance with the general spirit of his teachings, and
if he ever did make the statement reported it is probably
only one of those nonsensical utterances which he seems to
have occasionally made, solely for the purpose of having a
long string of short sentences. The statement in question
is even on Chu Hai's interpretation absurd and impossible.

In their views about death, also, our two sages seem to
have been much alike. They do not refer to a state of
existence hereafter, and they seem to have regarded the
grave as the end of man, so far as his consciousness of being
was concerned, at least. On this subject, however, we must
speak with caution as the utterances of both are few and
dark.

2 For the duty of self-denial at certain times see the Li-chi, ch. 3, p.
53, and Callery's Li-ki, p. 31.

3 The Great Learning. See Legge's Ch. Classics, vol. i., p. 222.

A few general observations will now conclude these rather disjointed remarks about the points of similarity in the Tao-tĕ Ching and the Confucian classics. The Chung-yung, or Constant Mean, called by Dr. Legge the Doctrine of the Mean, amplifies and illustrates several of Lao-tzŭ's teachings, and every reader of the book must have observed the frequency of the occurrence of the word Tao in it. The expression Chung-yung is, indeed, sometimes almost convertible with this word, and Confucius speaks of *keeping* it in terms very similar to those which Lao-tzŭ uses about Tao. Again, the Li (禮) of the Li-chi, Lun-Yü, and other works is a word of far wider and deeper signification than our translations usually represent. It seems often to indicate the carrying out of the theoretical Tao into practical life.[4] Several passages in the classic, named from the word, might be cited in support of the above view, and in one remarkable sentence, Confucius says that Li must have had its origin in the " Great One."[5] The Shu-ching, or Classic of historical excerpts, contains, as has been seen, many doctrines and sayings similar to those of the Tao-tĕ Ching, and a similar remark applies to the Yi-Ching, especially to its appendix. The collection of early moral and immoral ballads usually dignified by the title Shi-ching or Classic of poetry, as might have been expected, does not throw much light on the influence exercised by Lao-tzŭ over Confucius or the similarity of their teachings, and the same is true of the Ch'un-ch'iu (春秋) or Annals of his Dynasty by Con-

4 In the Li-chi, Confucius says that as a parrot does not cease to be a bird though it can speak, so though creatures have the appearance of men, yet if they have not Li they are not men. Ch. 1., p. 4.

5 Li-chi, ch. 4, p. 60.

fucius. Descending to Mencius we find in the sayings
recorded of him many doctrines very like some of Lao-tzŭ's,
and it is a remarkable fact that he never refers to the latter
either in praise or in dispraise. Later Confucianists have
regarded their Master as a born sage, and they would generally scout the idea that he was under serious obligations
to any one, and to Lao-tzŭ in particular.

While noticing the many points of affinity between Lao-
tzŭ and Confucius, we ought not to forget that there are at
the same time great and important differences between them.
The type of mind of the former does not very much resemble
that of the latter. Lao-tzŭ is chiefly synthetic and Confucius analytic in tendency. The former likes to sum
up particular virtues and existences, and refer them to one
all-embracing idea. The latter shows how one great principle branches off and becomes separated into many secondary
modes and finally permeates all things. The one is a philosopher at home, and the other a schoolmaster abroad. The
relation between the two may in some respects be compared
to that between Plato and Aristotle, if it be lawful to compare small things with great. The character of Plato's mind
also somewhat resembles that of Lao-tzŭ, while Aristotle is
very faintly foreshadowed in Confucius. He was a disciple of
Plato and yet he came to differ very widely from his master,
but not more than Confucius did from Lao-tzŭ. In both
cases the disciple became more practical and less theoretical
than his master. Yet it must be borne in mind that many
of Confucius' teachings in politics and morals are either
nonsensical or at least vague and incomprehensible, and that
Lao-tzŭ's general theories are not seldom applicable to
particulars and the actual world.

CHAPTER IX.

CONCLUSION.

It would be a very interesting study to examine the points of similarity and difference in the writings of the early Buddhists and the teachings of Lao-tzŭ; but this cannot be attempted here. There is one circumstance, however, to which I shall allude, that is, the resemblance of the Buddhist Bôdhisattva (P'usa) Mandjusri to Lao-tzŭ. The Nepaulese traditions about this P'usa also make him to be a foreigner and to have come to their country from China, though other accounts represent him as returning from the latter country to his home in Nepaul. A full and very interesting account of Mandjusri, or "Mañdjuçri," as Burnouf writes it, will be found in that accomplished scholar's " Le Lotus de la bonne Loi."[1] Rémusat and Pauthier insist on the western origin of Lao-tzŭ's doctrines, and there are certainly not a few points of resemblance between them and some of the early Indian systems of religion and philosophy. Of these the doctrine of annihilation, or at least of final absorption, is one of the most striking.

Another interesting study in connection with Lao-tzŭ

1 Page 498, &c.

would be to trace the history of his opinions among succeed-
ing generations. This would, however, be in a great degree
a painful study. The metaphysical work of Chwang-tzŭ,
wild and extravagant though it be occasionally, is worthy of
being read, and M. Julien has kindly promised to translate
it for us. Lie-tzŭ and several others of his followers are
also worth reading, but the great majority of so called
Taoist books are utterly despicable at least in our eyes. Mr
Edkins says of the "Taoist system"—"Its appeal is made
to the lower wants of the Chinese. It invents divinities to
promote the physical well-being of the people. The gods of
riches, of longevity, of war, and of particular disease, all
belong to this religion."[2] The pure and spiritual sayings
uttered by Lao-tzŭ have been taken in a gross sense
and perverted by thoughtless, faithless people, who would
have a meritorious life consist solely in external acts, thus
entirely reversing their master's precepts. He spoke of
length of days to be desired as the result of a calm and
philosophic life, but degenerate followers sought for many
years, in ways shameful to relate. They changed his plain
and simple language into euphuistic terms which cause them
to be reproached. The Taoists, says one author, call the
chattering of their teeth the Heavenly drum, they swallow
their spittle and call it the Fairy Spring, they speak of
horse's excrement as magical fuel and of rats as vivifying
medicine. By such means they think they can attain Tao,
but, as the writer asks,—can they attain it?[3]

Though his doctrines, however, have become greatly
corrupted and perverted the greatness of Lao-tzŭ himself

2 Religious Condition, &c., p. 68.
3 See the Yuan-chien, &c., ch. 319.

has not diminished. From the time of the Empress (姜)
of the West Hans, near the end of the Chou dynasty, the
beginning of his honour dates, and from the time of the
Chin and Liang dynasties down to the Great Tang dynasty,
his doctrines and his name were glorified."[4] He was promoted to be a God, and wonderful things were invented
about him and the *Tao* of which he spoke so much. One
of the Tang emperors conferred on him the sublime title—
Great Ruler of the very exalted mysterious Beginning.
Nor has he remained without honour among outside barba-
rians. Cunningham says :—"He (Lao-tzŭ) was therefore a
contemporary of Sakya Muni, by whom he is said to have
been worsted in argument. By the Tibetan Buddhists he
is called Sen-rabs ; but this perhaps signifies nothing more
than that he was of the race or family of Sena. His faith
continued paramount in Great Tibet for nine centuries,
until Buddhism was generally introduced by Seong-Stan
in the middle of the seventh century." It seems to me
more than doubtful, however, whether these Tirthikas of
India, to whom Cunningham alludes as the adherents of
Lao-tzŭ's faith, can be regarded as such. A large and influ-
ential school could not be established in so short a time as
elapsed between the time when Lao-tzŭ flourished and the
time of Buddha's preaching, if indeed any time whatever
elapsed. It is perhaps sufficient to observe that there is a
considerable amount of similarity between the tenets imputed
to the Tirthikas and those of the Chinese philosopher.

The followers of Lao-tzŭ spread his fame among the
Japanese islands also, where Sinto or Shên-tao, that is the

4 See Chu-bai's Tsa-cho, ch. 9.

5 Ladak, p. 358.

Spiritual Tao, was known before Buddhism was introduced.
Sir R. Alcock, however, says—"That there was an indi-
genous religion as old as their (the Japanese) history, one
formed by and for themselves in long past ages, the Sintoo,
which survives to this day; that some ten or fifteen centuries
ago or more, this was overlaid by the Confucian doctrines—
a code of moral ethics, not a religion in the proper sense
of the term—and about the seventh century both were in
great degree supplemented by the Buddhist faith derived from
China, we do know with tolerable certainty. But this is
nearly the sum."[6] Mr. Edkins has given a short but very
interesting account of Taoism in Japan, derived principally
from Kœmpfer. It is somewhat remarkable that as the
Japanese have their spiritual chief or Mikado so the Chinese
Taoists also have one, and each is supposed to be a present
deity having a sacred title derived through many ages.
The Chinese chief, however, is a much less powerful and
important personage than the Mikado. The first of the
Taoist patriarchs in China was Chang Tao-ling (張道陵)
who lived in the time of the Han dynasty.[7] Lao-tzŭ appeared
to him on the Stork-cry Hill and told him that in order ·
to attain the state of immortality which he was seeking he
must subdue a number of demons. Tao-ling in his eagerness
slew too many, and Lao-tzŭ told him that Shang Ti required
him to do penance for a time. Finally, however, he was
allowed to become an immortal, and the spiritual chiefdom
of the Taoists was given to his family for ever. The
descendants of Tao-ling reside at the Dragon-tiger Hill near
Kwei-hsi in the province of Kiangsi. It is apparently about

6 The Capital of the Tycoon, vol. ii., p. 258.
7 See for this man the 尚友錄, ch. 8.

this Chang Tao-ling that Edkins says—" Chang, one of the
genü of Taouist romance, is believed to be identical with the
star cluster of the same name, and he is represented by
painters and idol makers with a bow in his hands, shooting
the heavenly dog."[8]   One title of this spiritual chief in
China is Tien-shi, or Heavenly Teacher and the original
patriarch seems to be worshipped in Japan under this name.
Commodore Perry says that of the two und twenty shrines
in the kingdom which command the homage of pilgrimage,
" the great and most sacred one is that of the Sun-goddess,
Ten-sio-dai-sin, at Isye."   Previously he had stated—" It is
said that the only object of *worship* among the Sintoos is the
Sun-goddess, Ten-sio-dai-zin, who is deemed the patron
divinity of Japan * * * The Mikado is supposed to be her
lineal descendant."[9]   Why, however, the deity should be a
female and a Sun-goddess I do not understand.

   We must now bid farewell to Lao-tzŭ.   The study of his
work and his life, as also of the fortunes of his doctrines, is
a difficult task but not without interest and instruction, and
the writer is afraid he has lingered too long over it.   He
hopes, however, that his efforts will even in a very small
degree help to raise Lao-tzŭ to the place in the history of
Philosophy, and in the history of the benefactors of humanity,
to which he is fairly entitled.

8 Religious Condition, &c., p. 140.
9 American Expedition to Japan, ps. 24-5.

www.ingramcontent.com/pod-product-compliance
Lightning Source LLC
Chambersburg PA
CBHW030628270326
41927CB00007B/1349